STUDENT'S SOLUTIONS MANUAL

Miller and Freund's Probability and Statistics for Engineers

Fifth Edition

Richard A. Johnson
University of Wisconsin–Madison

Prentice Hall, Englewood Cliffs, New Jersey 07632

Editorial/ production supervision: ***Barbara Christenberry***
Production Coordinator: ***Trudy Pisciotti***
Acquisitions editor: ***Priscilla McGeehon***

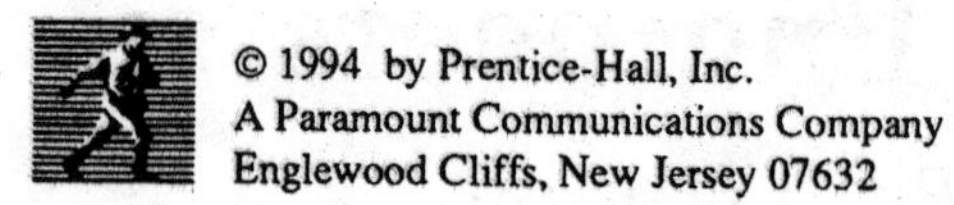

A Paramount Communications Company
Englewood Cliffs, New Jersey 07632

Printed in the United States of America

10 9 8 7 6 5 4 3 2 1

ISBN 0-13-721416-2

Prentice-Hall International (UK) Limited, London
Prentice-Hall of Australia Pty. Limited, Sydney
Prentice-Hall Canada Inc. Toronto
Prentice-Hall Hispanoamericana, S.A., Mexico
Prentice-Hall of India Private Limited, New Delhi
Prentice-Hall of Japan, Inc., Tokyo
Simon & Schuster Asia Pte. Ltd., Singapore
Editora Prentice-Hall do Brasil, Ltda., Rio de Janeiro

TABLE OF CONTENTS

CONTENTS

PREFACE

This student's manual is intended to help the student gain an improved understanding of the subject by providing model solutions for one fourth of all of the exercises in the text. The first exercises in the book appear in Chapter 2 and the chapters in this manual are numbered accordingly.

In the spirit of quality improvement, we would appreciate receiving your comments, corrections and suggestions for improvements.

Richard A. Johnson

Chapter 2

TREATMENT OF DATA

2.1 Pareto chart of the accident data

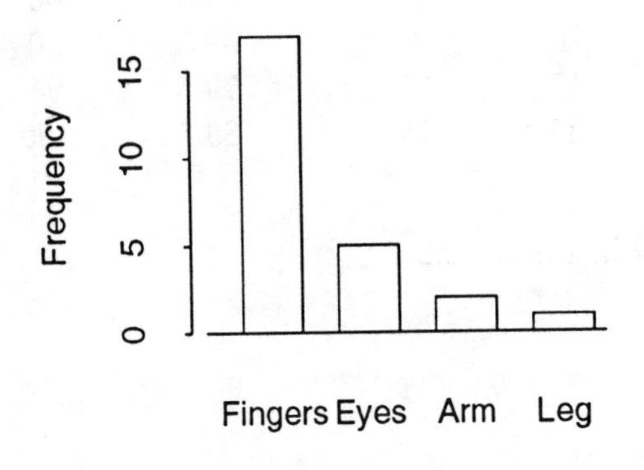

Figure 2.1: Pareto chart for Exercise 2.1

2.5 a) The class marks are 10.95, 11.95, 12.95, and 13.95

b) The class boundaries are:

10.45–11.45, 11.45–12.45, 12.45–13.45, 13.45–14.45.

c) The class interval is 1.

2.9 a) The class boundaries are symmetric around the class marks, and all but the two most extreme are given by the mid-points between the class marks. Thus, the class boundaries are

11.5–20.5, 20.5–29.5, 29.5–38.5, 38.5–47.5, 47.5–56.5, 56.5–65.5.

b) The class limits are

12–20, 21–29, 30–38, 39–47, 48–56, 57–65.

2.13 The "less than" distribution of the data in the preceeding exercise is:

Class boundary	Count	Percent	Class boundary	Count	Percent
19.5	0	0	59.5	60	60
29.5	4	4	69.5	80	80
39.5	17	17	79.5	94	94
49.5	35	35	89.5	100	100

The ogive is plotted in Figure 2.2.

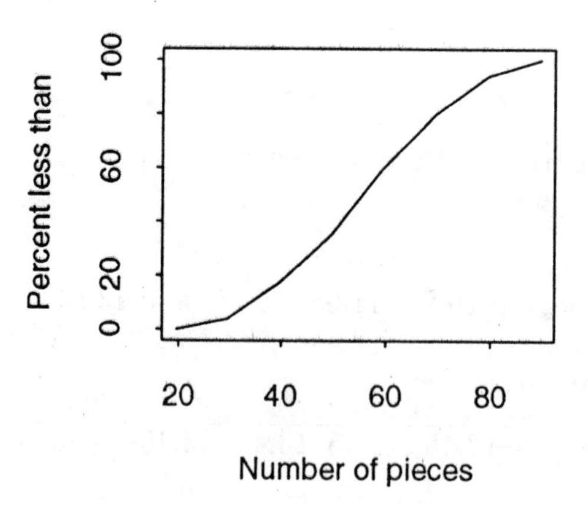

Figure 2.2: Ogive for Exercise 2.13

2.17 No. We tend to compare areas visually. The area of the large sack is far more than double the area of the small sack. The large sack should be modified so that its area is double that of the small sack.

2.21 The stem and leaf display is:

1**	
2**	67, 88, 95
3**	55, 70, 91, 83, 17
4**	05, 19, 34, 62
5**	40, 08
6**	12
7**	

2.25 (a) The mean is:

$$\frac{33+24+39+48+26+35+38+54+23+34+29+37}{12} = 35$$

(b) Sorting the data gives:

23, 24, 26, 29, 33, 34, 35, 37, 38, 39, 48, 54.

The median is the average of the sixth and seventh smallest observations or

$(34 + 35)/2 = 34.5$.

2.29 (a) The mean is 8.

(b) The sorted data are:

1, 2, 2, 3, 5, 6, 8, 9, 9, 10, 10, 10, 13, 15, 17.

The median is the eighth smallest which is 9.

(c) The boxplot is given in Figure 2.3.

2.33 $\sum x_i = 6,046$ $\sum x_i^2 = 2,569,836$. Thus,

$s^2 = (15 \cdot 2569836 - 6046^2)/(15 \cdot 14) = 9492.5.$ and $s = 97.43$.

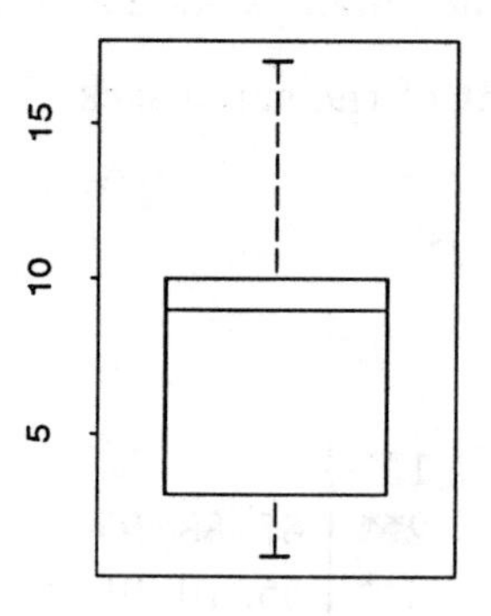

Figure 2.3: Boxplot for Exercise 2.29

2.37 (a) $\sum x_i = 605$. Thus, $\bar{x} = 605/20 = 30.25$, and $\sum x_i^2 = 20,663$. Hence, $s^2 = (20 \cdot 21723 - 615^2)/(20 \cdot 19) = 124.303$. And $s = 11.15$.

(b) The class limits, marks, and frequencies are in the following table:

Class limits	Class mark	Frequency
10–19	14.5	3
20–29	24.5	8
30–39	34.5	5
40–49	44.5	3
50–59	54.5	1

Thus,

$\bar{x} = (3(14.5) + 8(24.5) + 5(34.5) + 3(44.5) + 54.5)/20 = 30.$

$\sum x_i f_i = 600.$ $\sum x_i^2 f_i = 20,295.$ Thus ,

$s^2 = (20 \cdot 20,295 - 600^2)/(20 \cdot 19) = 120.79.$ So, $s = 10.99.$

2.41 Let x_i be the copper prices, and y_i be the coal prices. then, $\bar{x} = 67.57$ and $s_{copper} = 1.779$. Thus, $V_{copper} = 2.63$ percent. Now $\bar{y} = 20.55$ and $s_{coal} = 1.614$. Thus, $V_{coal} = 7.85$ percent. Thus, coal prices are relatively more variable.

2.45 (a) The median is the average of the 25'th and 26'th largest observations. These values are in the third class (10 - 14) which has frequency 16. The lower class boundary is 9.5 and the class interval is 5. There are 19 observations in the lower two classes. Thus, the estimate for the median is $5(50/2 - 19)/16 + 9.5 = 11.375$.

(b) There are 60 observations. The median falls in the third class (25.0 - 29.9) which has frequency 24. There are 18 observations in the lower two classes. The lower class boundary is 24.95 and the class interval is 5. Thus, the estimate for the median is $5(60/2 - 18)/24 + 24.95 = 27.45$.

(c) There are 80 observations. There are 40 observations in the first four classes, and 40 in the last four. Thus, the estimate for the median is the class boundary between the 4'th and 5'th class or 4.995.

2.49 (a) The weighted average for the student is

$(69 + 75 + 56 + 72 + 4 \cdot 78)/8 = 73.0$.

(b) The combined percent increase for the average salaried worker is:

$(28 \cdot 53 + 35 \cdot 40 + 14 \cdot 34)/(28 + 35 + 14) = 43.64$ percent.

2.53 (a) The frequency table of the aluminum alloy strength data is

Class limits	Frequency
66.0–67.4	1
67.5–68.9	8
69.0–70.4	19
70.5–71.9	17
72.0–73.4	9
73.5–74.9	3
75.0–76.4	1

(b) The histogram, using the frequency table in part (a), is shown in Figure 2.4.

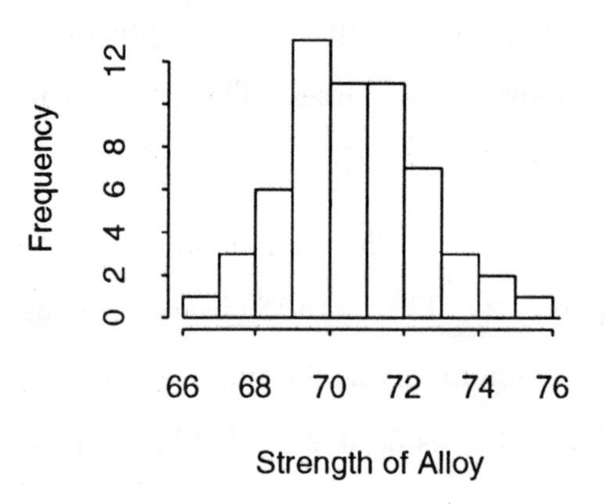

Figure 2.4: Histogram for Exercise 2.53

2.57 (a) The ordered data are:

0.32 0.34 0.40 0.40 0.43 0.48 0.57

Since there are 7 observations, the median is the middle value. The median, maximum, minimum and range for the Tube 1 observations are:

Median = 0.40, maximum = 0.57, minimum = 0.32 and

range = maximum − minimum = 0.57 − 0.32 = 0.25.

(b) The ordered data are:

0.47 0.47 0.48 0.51 0.53 0.61 0.63

And the median, maximum, minimum and range for the Tube 2 observations are:

Median = 0.51, maximum = 0.63, minimum = 0.47 and

range = maximum − minimum = 0.63 − 0.47 = 0.16.

2.61 (a) The ordered data are:

12 14 19 20 21 28 29 30 55 63 63

The quartiles for the suspended solids data are $Q_1 = 19$ and $Q_3 = 55$.

(b) The minimum, maximum, range and the interquartile range are

Minimum = 12, maximum = 63, range = 63 − 12 = 51 and

interquartile range = $Q_3 - Q_1 = 55 - 19 = 36$.

(c) The boxplot appears in Figure 2.5.

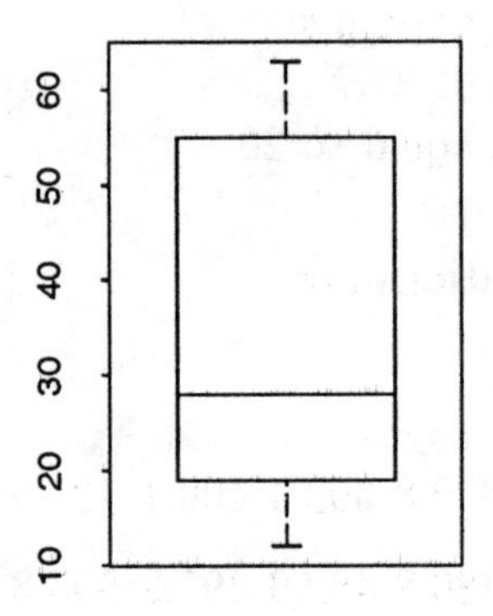

Figure 2.5: Boxplot for Exercise 2.61

2.65 The table might look like

Class limits	Frequency	Class limits	Frequency
1160–1179		1240–1259	
1180–1199		1260–1279	
1200–1219		1280–1299	
1220–1239		1300–1319	

The section for "tally" and "frequency" have not been filled in because we have not been given the actual data.

(a) The class limits are given in the table.

(b) The class marks are given by the average of successive class limits or boundaries and they are 1169.5, 1189.5, 1209.5, 1229.5, 1249.5, 1269.5, 1289.5, 1309.5.

(c) The class boundaries are

1159.5–1179.5, 1179.5–1199.5, 1199.5–1219.5,

1219.5–1239.5, 1239.5–1259.5, 1259.5–1279.5,

1279.5–1299.5, 1299.5–1319.5.

(d) The class interval is equal to 20.

2.69 (a) The ordered observations are

389.1 390.8 392.4 400.1 425.9 429.1 448.4 461.6
479.1 480.8 482.9 497.2 505.8 516.5 517.5 547.5
550.9 563.7 567.7 572.2 572.5 575.6 595.5 602.0
606.7 611.9 618.9 626.9 634.9 644.0 657.6 679.3
698.6 718.5 738.0 743.3 752.6 760.6 794.8 817.2
833.9 889.0 895.8 904.7 986.4 1146.0 1156.0

The first quartile is the 12th observation, 497.2, the median is the 24th observation, 602.0, and the third quartile is the 36th observation, 743.3.

(b) Since $47(.90) = 42.3$, the 90th percentile is the 43rd observation, 895.8.

(c) The histogram is

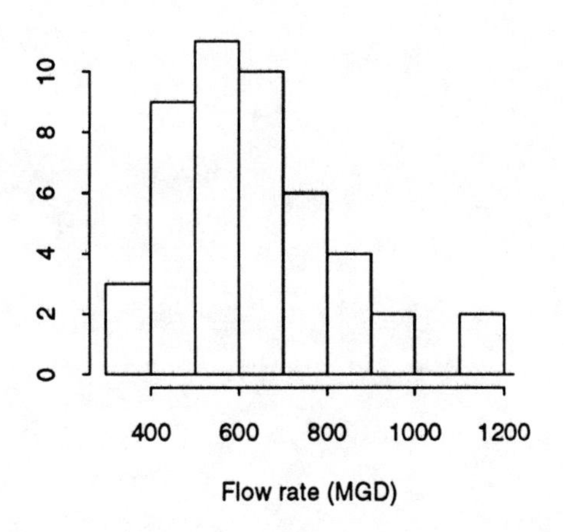

Figure 2.6: Histogram for Exercise 2.69(c).

Chapter 3

PROBABILITY

3.1 (a) A sketch of the 12 points of the sample space is as follows:

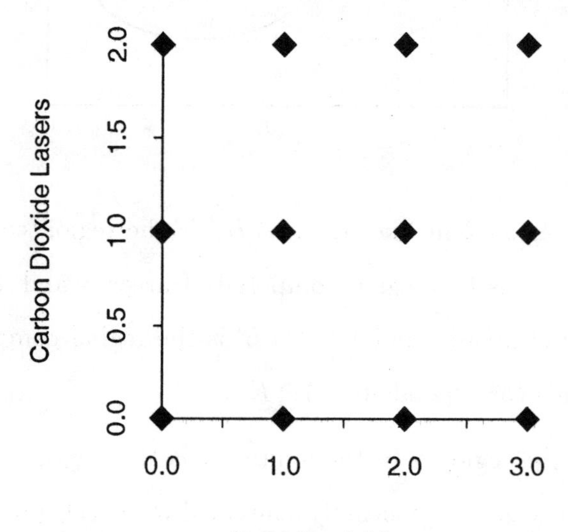

(b) R={(0,0),(1,1),(2,2)}. T={(0,0),(1,0),(2,0),(3,0)}. U={(0,1),(0,2),(1,2)}.

3.5 A={3,4}, B={2,3}, C={4,5}.

(a) $A \cup B$={2,3,4}. Work is easy, average or difficult on this model.

(b) $A \cap B$={3}. Work is average on this model.

(c) B'={1,4,5}. Thus $A \cup B'$={1,3,4,5}. Work is not easy on this model.

(d) C'={1,2,3}. Work is very easy, easy or average on this model.

3.9 Region 1 is the event that the ore contains both uranium and copper. Region 2 is the event that the ore contains copper but not uranium. Region 3 is the event that the ore contains uranium but not copper. Region 4 is the event that the ore contains neither uranium nor copper.

3.13 The following Venn diagram will be used in parts (a), (b), (c) and (d).

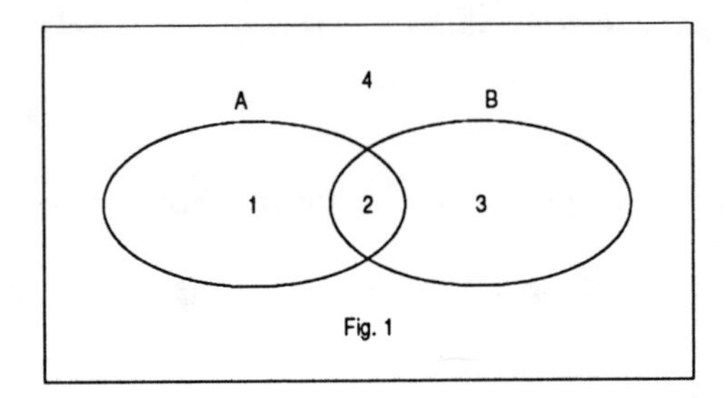

Fig. 1

(a) $A \cap B$ is region 2 in Fig. 1. $(A \cap B)'$ is the region composed of areas 1, 3, and 4. A' is the region composed of areas 3 and 4. B' is the region composed of areas 1 and 4. $A' \cup B'$ is the region composed of areas 1, 3, and 4. This corresponds to $(A \cap B)'$.

(b) $A \cap B$ is the region 2 in the figure. A is the region composed of areas 1 and 2. Since $A \cap B$ is entirely contained in A, $A \cup (A \cap B) = A$.

(c) $A \cap B$ is region 2. $A \cap B'$ is region 1. Thus, $(A \cap B) \cup (A \cap B')$ is the region composed of areas 1 and 2 which is A.

(d) From part (c), we have $(A \cap B) \cup (A \cap B') = A$. Thus, we must show that $(A \cap B) \cup (A \cap B') \cup (A' \cap B) = A \cup (A' \cap B) = A \cup B$. A is the region composed of areas 1 and 2 and $A' \cap B$ is region 3. Thus, $A \cup (A' \cap B)$ is the region composed of areas 1, 2, and 3.

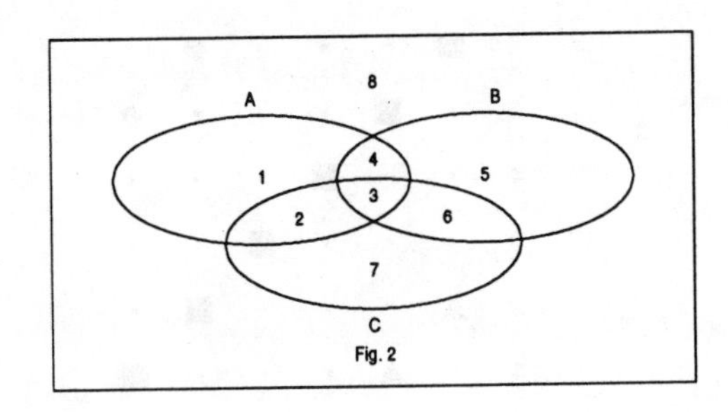

Fig. 2

(e) In Fig. 2, $A \cup B$ is the region composed of areas 1, 2, 3, 4, 5, and 6. $A \cup C$ is the region composed of areas 1, 2, 3, 4, 6, and 7, so $(A \cup B) \cap (A \cup C)$ is the region composed of areas 1, 2, 3, 4, and 6. $B \cap C$ is the region composed of areas 3, and 6, and A is the region composed of areas 1, 2, 3, and 4. Thus, $A \cup (B \cap C)$ is the region composed of areas 1, 2, 3, 4, and 6. Thus $A \cup (B \cap C) = (A \cup B) \cap (A \cup C)$.

3.17 There are $(6)(4)(3) = 72$ ways.

3.21 $6! = 720$.

3.25 There are ${}_{12}C_3 = 220$ ways to draw the three recharageable batteries. There are ${}_{11}C_3 = 165$ ways to draw none are defective.

(a) The number of ways to get the one that is defective is $220 - 165 = 55$.

(b) There are 165 ways not to get the one that is defective.

3.29 The outcome space is given in Figure 3.1.

(a) The 6 outcomes summing to 7 are marked by squares. Thus, the probability is $6/36 = 1/6$.

(b) There are 2 outcomes summing to 11, which are marked by diamonds. Thus, the probability is $2/36 = 1/18$.

(c) These events are mutually exclusive. Thus, the probability is $6/36+2/36 = 2/9$.

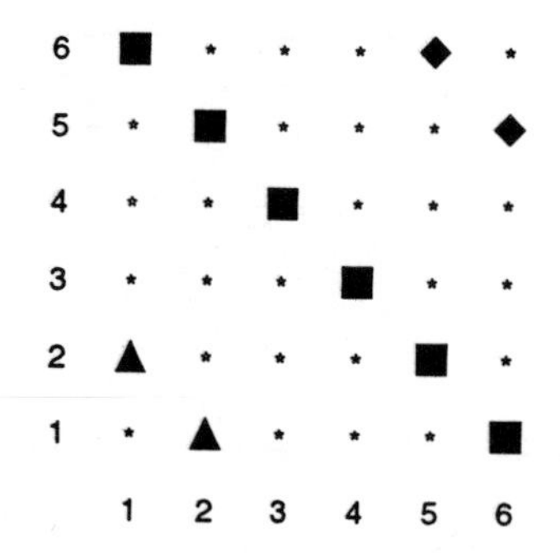

Figure 3.1: The outcome space for Exercise 3.29.

(d) The 2 outcomes are marked by triangles. Thus, the probability is $2/36 = 1/18$.

(e) There are two such outcomes, (1,1) and (6,6). Thus, the probability is $2/36 = 1/18$.

(f) There are four such outcomes, (1,1), (1,2), (2,1) and (6,6). Thus, the probability is $4/36 = 1/9$.

3.33 The number of students enrolled in the statistics course or the operations research course is $92 + 63 - 40 = 115$. Thus, $160 - 115 = 45$ are not enrolled in either course.

3.37 (a) There is 1 point where $i+j = 2$. There are 2 points where $i+j = 3$. There are 2 points where $i+j = 4$. There is 1 point where $i+j = 5$. Thus,

$$\begin{aligned}\frac{15/28}{2} + 2 \cdot \frac{15/28}{3} + 2 \cdot \frac{15/28}{4} + \frac{15/28}{5} \\ = \frac{15}{28} \cdot (1/2 + 2/3 + 1/2 + 1/5) = \frac{15}{28} \cdot \frac{28}{15} = 1.\end{aligned}$$

Since each probability is between 0 and 1, the assignment is permissible.

(b) $P(B) = 15/28 \cdot (1/4 + 1/5) = 5/28 \cdot 9/20 = 135/560 = 27/112$.

$P(C) = 15/28 \cdot (1/2 + 1/4) = 15/28 \cdot 3/4 = 45/112$.

$P(D) = 15/28 \cdot (1/3 + 1/3) = 15/28 \cdot 2/3 = 5/14.$

(c) The probability that 1 graduate student will be supervising the lab is:

$$\frac{15/28}{2} + \frac{15/28}{3} = \frac{25}{56} = .446.$$

The probability that 2 graduate students will be supervising the lab is:

$$\frac{15/28}{3} + \frac{15/28}{4} = \frac{35}{112} = \frac{5}{16} = .3125.$$

The probability that 3 graduate students will be supervising the lab is:

$$\frac{15/28}{4} + \frac{15/28}{5} = \frac{27}{112} = .241.$$

3.41 (a) $P(A') = 1 - P(A) = 1 - .29 = .71.$

(b) $P(A \cup B) = P(A) + P(B) = .29 + .43 = .72$, since A and B are mutually exclusive.

(c) $P(A \cap B') = P(A) = .29$, since A and B are mutually exclusive.

(d) $P(A' \cap B') = P((A \cup B)') = 1 - P(A \cap B) = 1 - .29 - .43 = .28.$

3.45 (a) 15/32 (b) 13/32 (c) 5/32 (d) 23/32 (e) 8/32 (f) 9/32.

3.49

$P(A \cup B \cup C) = 1 - .11 = .89,$ $\quad P(A) = .24 + .06 + .04 + .16 = .5,$

$P(B) = .19 + .06 + .04 + .11 = .4,$ $\quad P(C) = .09 + .16 + .04 + .11 = .4,$

$P(A \cap B) = .06 + .04 = .1,$ $\quad P(A \cap C) = .16 + .04 = .2,$

$P(B \cap C) = .04 + .11 = .15,$ $\quad P(A \cap B \cap C) = .04.$

Thus, the following equation must equal to .89:

$$.5 + .4 + .4 - .1 - .2 - .15 + .04 = .89.$$

This verifies the formula.

3.53 (a) $p = 3/(3+2) = 3/5$.

(b) $30/(30+10) = 3/4 \leq p < 40/(10+40) = 4/5$.

3.57 (a) The sample space is C. Thus the probability is given by:

$$\frac{N(A \cap C)}{N(C)} = \frac{8+15}{8+54+9+14} = \frac{62}{85} = .73.$$

(b) This is given by:

$$\frac{N(A \cap B)}{N(A)} = \frac{20+54}{20+54+8+2} = \frac{74}{84} = .881.$$

(c) This is given by:

$$\frac{N(C' \cap B')}{N(B')} = \frac{N((C \cup B)')}{N(B')} = \frac{150-121}{105-99} = \frac{29}{51} = .569.$$

3.61 $P(A|B) = P(A \cap B)/P(B)$ by definition. Thus, $P(A|B) = P(A)$ implies $P(A \cap B)/P(B) = P(A)$, which implies $P(A \cap B)/P(A) = P(B)$, since both $P(A)$ and $P(B)$ are not zero. Thus $P(B|A) = P(B)$.

3.65 (a) The probability of drawing a Seattle-bound part on the first draw is 45/60. The probability of drawing a Seattle-bound part on the second draw given that a Seattle-bound part was drawn on the first draw is 44/59. Thus, the probability that both parts should have gone to Seattle is:

$$\frac{45}{60} \cdot \frac{44}{59} = .559.$$

(b) Using an approach similar to (a), the probability that both parts should have gone to Vancouver is:

$$\frac{15}{60} \cdot \frac{14}{59} = .059.$$

(c) The probability that one should have gone to Seattle and one to Vancouver is 1 minus the sum of the probability in parts (a) and (b) or .381.

3.69 (a) Each head has probability 1/2, and each toss is independent. Thus, the probability of 8 heads is $(1/2)^8 = 1/256$.

(b) $P(\text{three 3's and then a 4 or 5}) = (1/6)^3(1/3) = 1/648$.

(c) $P(\text{five questions answered correctly}) = (1/3)^5 = 1/243$.

3.73 $P(\text{car had bad tires}) = (.20)(.10)+(.20)(.12)+(.60)(.04)=.068$.

3.77 (a)

$$\begin{aligned} &P(\text{Tom} \mid \text{Incomplete repair}) \\ &= \frac{(.6)(1/10)}{(.2)(1/20) + (.6)(1/10) + (.15)(1/10) + (.05)(1/20)} \\ &= \frac{.06}{.0875} = .686. \end{aligned}$$

(b)

$$P(\text{George} \mid \text{Incomplete repair}) = \frac{(.15)(1/10)}{.0875} = .171.$$

(c)

$$P(\text{Peter} \mid \text{Incomplete repair}) = \frac{(.05)(1/20)}{.0875} = .0286.$$

3.81 The expected gain is $(10)(1/2) + (-10)(1/2) = 0$ dollars.

3.85 If 6 items are stocked, the cost is (6)(35)=\$210. The expected revenue is:

$$(3.50)(.05) + (4.50)(.12) + (5.50)(.20) + (6.50)(.24 + .17 + .14 + .08) = \$270.5.$$

Thus, the expected profit is \$270.5−\$210=\$60.50.

If 7 items are stocked, the cost is (7)(35)=\$245. The expected revenue is:

$$(3.50)(.05)+(4.50)(.12)+(5.50)(.20)+(6.50)(.24)+(7.50)(.17+.14+.08) = \$290.$$

Thus, the expected profit is \$290−\$245=\$45.

3.89 (a) He feels that $p(-1.20) + (1 - p)(1.20) < .80$, where p is the probability that a person will ask for double his money back. Thus, $p > 1/6$.

(b) Changing the direction of the inequalities in part (a) gives $p < 1/6$.

(c) Changing the inequalities in part (a) to equalities gives p=1/6.

3.93 Now, the expected gain if they continue is

$$(\$1,000,000)(.20) - (\$600,000)(.80) = -\$280,000.$$

If they do not continue, the expected gain is

$$(-\$400,000)(.20) + (\$100,000)(.80) = \$0.$$

They should not continue the operation.

3.94 If they spend \$300,000 and wait, the expected gain is

$$(1,000,000 - 300,00)(.4) + (100,000 - 300,000)(.6) = \$160,000.$$

It would be worthwhile to spend the addition funds.

3.97 (a) $X' = \{(0,0),(0,1),(0,2),(0,3),(1,0),(1,1),(1,2),(2,0),(2,1),(3,0)\}$.

X' is the event that the salesman will not visit all four of his customers.

(b) $X \cup Y = \{(4,0),(3,1),(2,2),(1,3),(0,4),(1,0),(2,0),(2,1),(3,0)\}$.

$X \cup Y$ is the event that the salesman will visit all four customers or more on the first day than on the second day.

(c) $X \cap Z = \{(1,3),(0,4)\}$.

$X \cap Z$ is the event that he will visit all four customers but at most one on the first day.

(d) $X' \cap Y = \{(1,0),(2,0),(2,1),(3,0)\}$.

$X' \cap Y$ is the event that he will visit at most three of the customers and more on the first day than on the second day.

3.101 There are ${}_7C_2 = 21$ ways to assign the chemical engineers.

3.105 The total number of employees that got a raise or an increase in pension benefits is $312 + 248 - 173 = 387$. If 43 got neither, then there must be $387 + 43 = 430$ employees, not 400 employees.

3.109 Let events S.E. = static electricity, E = explosion, M = malfunction, O.F. = open flame, and P.A. = purposeful action. We need to find probabilities P(S.E.|E), P(M|E), P(O.F.|E), P(P.A.|E). Since

$$P(E) = (.30)(.25) + (.40)(.20) + (.15)(.40) + (.15)(.75) = .3275,$$

we have

$$P(S.E.|E) = (.30)(.25)/.3275 = .229, \qquad P(M|E) = (.40)(.20)/.3275 = .244,$$

$$P(O.F.|E) = (.15)(.40)/.3275 = .183, \qquad P(P.A.|E) = (.15)(.75)/.3275 = .344.$$

Thus, purposeful action is most likely.

Chapter 4

PROBABILITY DISTRIBUTIONS

4.1 Let N be the number of suitable lasers.

$$P(N=0) = 1/2 \qquad P(N=3) = 3/12 = 1/4$$
$$P(N=1) = 2/12 = 1/6 \qquad P(N=4) = 2/12 = 1/6$$
$$P(N=2) = 3/12 = 1/4 \qquad P(N=5) = 1/12.$$

Thus, the distribution can be tabulated as :

N	0	1	2	3	4	5
Prob	1/12	1/6	1/4	1/4	1/6	1/12

4.5 Using the identity

$$(x-1)\sum_{i=0}^{n} x^i = x^{n+1} - 1$$

or

$$\sum_{i=0}^{n} x^i = \frac{x^{n+1}-1}{x-1},$$

we have

$$\sum_{x=0}^{4} \frac{k}{2^x} = k\frac{(\frac{1}{2})^{4+1}-1}{\frac{1}{2}-1} = \frac{31k}{16}.$$

This must equal 1, so $k = 16/31$.

4.9

$$b(x+1;n,p) = \binom{n}{x+1} p^{x+1}(1-p)^{n-x-1}$$

and

$$b(x;n,p) = \binom{n}{x} p^{x}(1-p)^{n-x}$$

Therefore,

$$\frac{b(x+1;n,p)}{b(x;n,p)} = \frac{\binom{n}{x+1} p^{x+1}(1-p)^{n-x-1}}{\binom{n}{x} p^{x}(1-p)^{n-x}} = \frac{(n-x)p}{(x+1)(1-p)}$$

To Use the recursion for $n = 6$, $p = .3$, we first calculate

$$b(0;6,.3) = (.7)^6 = .1176.$$

Then,

$$b(1;6,.3) = \frac{(.3)6}{(.7)1} \cdot (.1176) = .3025$$

$$b(2;6,.3) = \frac{(.3)5}{(.7)2} \cdot (.3025) = .3241$$

$$b(3;6,.3) = \frac{(.3)4}{(.7)3} \cdot (.3241) = .1852$$

$$b(4;6,.3) = \frac{(.3)3}{(.7)4} \cdot (.1852) = .0595$$

$$b(5;6,.3) = \frac{(.3)2}{(.7)5} \cdot (.0595) = .0102$$

$$b(6;6,.3) = \frac{(.3)1}{(.7)6} \cdot (.0102) = .0007$$

These values do check with those obtained by differencing the entries in Table 1.

4.13

$$b(2;4,.75) = \binom{4}{2} (.75)^2(.25)^{4-2} = .2109.$$

4.17 (a) $P(18 \text{ are ripe}) = (.9)^{18} = .1501.$

(b) $1 - B(15;\ 18,\ .9) = 1 - .2662 = .7338.$

(c) $B(14;\ 18,\ .9) = .0982.$

4.21 For this problem, we need to use the hypergeometric distribution. The probability is given by:

$$h(2;6,8,18) = \frac{\binom{8}{2}\binom{10}{4}}{\binom{18}{6}} = \frac{(8!)\ (10!)\ (12!)}{2\ (6!)\ (4!)\ (18!)} = .3167$$

4.25 (a)

$$P(\text{none in west}) = h(0;3,7,16) = \frac{\binom{7}{0}\binom{9}{3}}{\binom{16}{3}} = \frac{1 \cdot 84}{560} = .15$$

(b)

$$P(\text{all in west}) = h(3; 3, 7, 16) = \frac{\binom{7}{3}\binom{9}{0}}{\binom{16}{3}} = \frac{35 \cdot 1}{560} = .0625$$

4.29 The cumulative binomial probabilities are

```
    CDF;
    BINOMIAL n = 27 p = .47 .

  BINOMIAL WITH N =   27   P = 0.470000
     K  P( X LESS OR = K)
     2          0.0000
     3          0.0001
     4          0.0005
     5          0.0021
     6          0.0072
     7          0.0210
     8          0.0515
     9          0.1086
    10          0.1998
    11          0.3247
    12          0.4724
    13          0.6236
    14          0.7576
    15          0.8607
    16          0.9292
    17          0.9685
    18          0.9879
    19          0.9960
    20          0.9989
    21          0.9997
    22          1.0000
```

4.33 Using the computing formula:

$$\sigma^2 = \mu_2' - \mu^2, \qquad \mu = 1.8$$

$$\mu_2' = 0^2(.17) + 1^2(.29) + 2^2(.27) + 3^2(.16) + 4^2(.07) + 5^2(.03) + 6^2(.01) = 5.04$$

Thus,

$$\sigma^2 = 5.04 - (1.8)^2 = 1.8.$$

The standard deviation is $\sigma = \sqrt{1.8} = 1.34$.

4.37 (a) The variance is given by:

$$\sigma^2 = (0-2.5)^2\frac{1}{32} + (1-2.5)^2\frac{5}{32} + (2-2.5)^2\frac{10}{32} + (3-2.5)^2\frac{10}{32}$$

$$+(4-2.5)^2\frac{5}{32} + (5-2.5)^2\frac{1}{32} = \frac{40}{32} = 1.25$$

(b) To use the computing formula we need:

$$\mu_2' = 0^2 \cdot \frac{1}{32} + 1^2 \cdot \frac{5}{32} + 2^2 \cdot \frac{10}{32} + 3^2 \cdot \frac{10}{32} + 4^2 \cdot \frac{5}{32} + 5^2 \cdot \frac{1}{32} = \frac{240}{32} = 7.5$$

Thus

$$\sigma^2 = 7.5 - (2.5)^2 = 1.25.$$

(c) The special formula for the binomial variance is:

$$\sigma^2 = np(1-p) = 5(.5)(.5) = 1.25$$

4.41 The mean of the hypergeometric distribution is

$$\begin{aligned}
\mu &= \sum_{x=0}^{n} x \frac{\binom{a}{x}\binom{N-a}{n-x}}{\binom{N}{n}} \\
&= \sum_{x=1}^{n} \frac{x\binom{a}{x}\binom{N-a}{n-x}}{\binom{N}{n}} \\
&= \frac{a}{\binom{N}{n}} \sum_{x=1}^{n} \binom{a-1}{x-1}\binom{N-a}{n-x}
\end{aligned}$$

Let $u = x - 1$. Then,

$$\mu = \frac{a}{\binom{N}{n}} \sum_{u=0}^{n-1} \binom{a-1}{u}\binom{N-a}{n-1-u}$$

Using the identity given in the problem, we have

$$\mu = \frac{a\binom{N-1}{n-1}}{\binom{N}{n}} = \frac{an}{N}$$

The result holds for all n such that $0 \le n \le N$, because

$$\binom{a}{x}\binom{N-a}{n-x} = 0 \quad \text{if} \quad x > a \quad \text{or} \quad (n-x) > (N-a)$$

4.45

$$\mu = 1,000,000 \cdot \frac{1}{2} = 500,000.$$

$$\sigma^2 = 1,000,000 \cdot \frac{1}{2} \cdot \frac{1}{2} = 250,000 \quad , \quad \sigma = 500.$$

If the proportion is between .495 and .505, the number of heads must be between 495,000 and 505,000. These bounds are both within 10 standard deviations of the mean. We can apply Chebyshev's theorem with $k = 10$. Thus, the probability is greater than $1 - 1/100 = .99$.

4.49 For $\lambda = 3$, $f(0;\lambda) = e^{-3} = .0498$. Thus, using

$$f(x+1;\lambda) = \frac{\lambda}{x+1} f(x;\lambda)$$

$$f(1;\lambda) = \frac{\lambda}{0+1} f(0;\lambda) = 3e^{-3} = .1494.$$

$$f(2;\lambda) = \frac{3}{2} \cdot 3e^{-3} = .2240.$$

and so forth. The values are given in the following table:

x	0	1	2	3	4
$f(x;3)$	.0498	.1494	.2240	.2240	.1680

x	5	6	7	8	9
$f(x;3)$	.1008	.0504	.0216	.0081	.0027

The probability histogram is given in Figure 4.1.

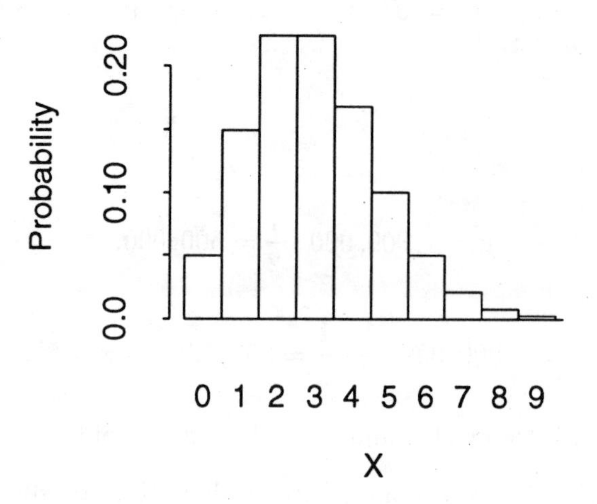

Figure 4.1: Probability Histogram for Exercise 4.49.

4.53 (a) $n = 80$, $p = .06$, $np = 4.8$. Thus,

$$f(4; 8.4) = F(4; 4.8) - F(3; 4.8) = (.476) - (.294) = .182$$

(b) $1 - F(2; 4.8) = 1 - (.143) = .857$

(c)

$$\sum_{k=3}^{6} f(k; 4.8) = F(6; 4.8) - F(2; 4.8) = (.791) - (.143) = .648$$

4.57 (a) $P(\text{at most 4 in a minute}) = F(4;\ 1.5\ ) = .981$.

(b) $P(\text{at least 3 in 2 minutes}) = 1 - F(2; 3) = 1 - (.423) = .577$.

(c) $P(\text{at most 15 in 6 minutes}) = F(15; 9) = .978$.

4.61 P (fails after 1,200 times)

$$= \sum_{x=1201}^{\infty} (1-p)^{x-1} p = \frac{(1-p)^{1200}\, p}{1-(1-p)} = (1-p)^{1200}$$

where $p = .001$. Thus,

$$P(\text{fails after 1,200 times }) = (.999)^{1200} = .3010.$$

4.65 The expected number of trucks in the queue is $\mu = \alpha/(\alpha - \beta)$. When $\alpha = 2$ and $\beta = 3$, we have $\mu = 2$. Thus the expected cost per hour is $2 \cdot 15 = 30$. When $\alpha = 2$ and $\beta = 3.5$, $\mu = 1.333$. Thus the expected cost per hour is $(1.333)15 = 20$. For an 8-hour day the savings are 80 dollars so it is not worthwhile.

4.69

$$\begin{aligned}
\mu &= \sum_{x=0}^{\infty} x f(x,\lambda) = \sum_{x=0}^{\infty} x \,\frac{(\lambda)^x}{x!} e^{-\lambda} = \lambda \sum_{x=1}^{\infty} \frac{(\lambda)^{x-1}}{(x-1)!} e^{-\lambda} \\
&= \lambda \sum_{x=0}^{\infty} \frac{(\lambda)^x}{x!} e^{-\lambda} \;=\; \lambda \\
\mu_2' &= \sum_{x=0}^{\infty} x^2 f(x,\lambda) = \sum_{x=0}^{\infty} x^2 \,\frac{(\lambda)^x}{x!} e^{-\lambda} = \sum_{x=1}^{\infty} \frac{x(\lambda)^x}{(x-1)!} e^{-\lambda} \\
&= \lambda \sum_{x=0}^{\infty} (x+1) \frac{(\lambda)^x}{x!} e^{-\lambda} \;=\; \lambda(\lambda+1)
\end{aligned}$$

Thus,

$$\sigma^2 = \mu_2' - \mu^2 = \lambda(\lambda+1) - \lambda^2 = \lambda$$

4.73 To find this probability , we use the multinomial distribution with $n = 6$, $x_1 = 2$, $x_2 = 3$, $x_3 = 1$, $p_1 = 1/4$, $p_2 = 1/2$ and $p_3 = 1/4$, Thus the probability is given by

$$\frac{6!}{2!\;3!\;1!} \left(\frac{1}{4}\right)^2 \left(\frac{1}{2}\right)^3 \left(\frac{1}{4}\right)^1 = .117$$

4.77 We will use column 4 of Table 7 for this simulation. Omitting 0, 7, 8, and 9 gives:

Roll no.	1	2	3	4	5	6	7	8	9	10	11	12
Digit	6	2	5	5	1	6	3	5	6	2	6	2

Roll no.	13	14	15	16	17	18	19	20	21	22	23	24
Digit	2	4	3	3	4	5	5	3	4	2	6	1

Roll no.	25	26	27	28	28	30	31	32	33	34	35	36
Digit	3	4	2	3	4	6	5	4	1	5	2	5

Roll no.	37	38	39	40	41	42	43	44	45	46	47	48
Digit	2	4	4	6	1	5	4	1	3	5	6	4

Roll no.	49	50	51	52	53	54	55	56	57	58	59	60
Digit	6	6	6	1	2	5	1	5	1	6	4	3

Roll no.	61	62	63	64	65	66	67	68	69	70	71	72
Digit	4	1	1	5	2	5	4	5	4	4	5	5

Roll no.	73	74	75	76	77	78	79	80	81	82	83	84
Digit	4	5	2	5	4	6	3	4	2	1	1	5

Roll no.	85	86	87	88	89	90	91	92	93	94	95	96
Digit	1	5	1	6	5	6	3	2	2	3	6	1

Roll no.	97	98	99	100	101	102	103	104	105	106	107	108
Digit	2	6	2	1	2	2	6	5	5	2	1	6

Roll no.	109	110	111	112	113	114	115	116	117	118	119	120
Digit	3	1	4	2	6	3	3	1	3	6	6	1

Since the table ran out of random digits in column 4, we started over in column 8.

4.81 The solution is

```
    RANDOM 10 observations into C1;
    INTEGER 50 to 100.
    PRINT C1
 C1
72   56   57   76   72   67   71   90   86   52
```

4.85 (a)

$$b(3;8,.2) = \binom{8}{3} (.2)^3\,(.8)^5 = \frac{8!}{3!\,5!}\,(.2)^3\,(.8)^5 = .1468$$

(b) $B(3;8,.2) - B(2;8,.2) = .9437 - .7969 = .1468$

4.89 (a) The variance is given by:

$$\begin{aligned}\sigma^2 &= (0-1.2)^2(.216) + (1-1.2)^2(.432) + (2-1.2)^2(.288) + (3-1.2)^2(.064) \\ &= .72\end{aligned}$$

(b) Using the special formula for the binomial variance

$$\sigma^2 = np(1-p) = 3(.4)(.6) = .72$$

4.93 Since $(202 - 142)/12 = (142 - 82)/12 = 5$, we can apply Chebyshev's theorem with $k = 5$. Let X be the number of orders filled. Then,

$$P(X \le 82 \text{ or } X \ge 202) = P(|X - 142| \ge 5 \cdot 12) \le \frac{1}{25}$$

Thus,

$$P(82 < X < 202) > \frac{24}{25} = .96$$

4.97 (a) The random numbers are distributed in the following table:

Number of spills	Probability	Cumulative probability	Random numbers
0	.2466	.2466	0000–2465
1	.3452	.5918	2466–5917
2	.2417	.8335	5918–8334
3	.1128	.9463	8335–9462
4	.0395	.9858	9463–9857
5	.0111	.9969	9858–9968
6	.0026	.9995	9969–9994
6	.0005	1.0000	9995–9999

(b) Using columns 9-12 of the third page of Table 7 and starting from the 21st row, gives:

Day	1	2	3	4	5
Random no.	8353	6862	0717	2171	3763
No. of spills	3	2	0	0	1

Day	6	7	8	9	10
Random no.	1230	6120	3443	9014	4124
No. of spills	0	2	1	3	1

Day	11	12	13	14	15
Random no.	7299	0127	5056	0314	9869
No. of spills	2	0	1	0	5

Day	16	17	18	19	20
Random no.	6251	4972	1354	3695	8898
No. of spills	2	1	0	1	3

Day	21	22	23	24	25
Random no.	1516	8319	3687	6065	3123
No. of spills	0	2	1	2	1

Day	26	27	28	29	30
Random no.	4802	8030	6960	1127	7749
No. of spills	1	2	2	0	2

Chapter 5

PROBABILITY DENSITIES

5.1

$$f(x) = \begin{cases} 2e^{-2x} & \text{for } x > 0 \\ 0 & \text{elsewhere} \end{cases}$$

Since e^{-2x} is always positive, $f(x)$ is always ≥ 0.

$$\int_{-\infty}^{\infty} f(x)dx = -e^{-2x}\Big|_0^{\infty} = 1$$

Thus, $f(x)$ is a density.

5.5

$$F(x) = \int_{-\infty}^{x} f(s)ds = \begin{cases} 0 & x < 0 \\ x^2/2 & 0 \leq x \leq 1 \\ 1/2 + [2s - s^2/2]\big|_1^x & 1 < x \leq 2 \\ 1 & x > 2 \end{cases}$$

$$= \begin{cases} 0 & x < 0 \\ x^2/2 & 0 \leq x \leq 1 \\ 2x - x^2/2 - 1 & 1 < x \leq 2 \\ 1 & x > 2 \end{cases}$$

(a) $P(X > 1.8) = 1 - F(1.8) = 1 - [2(1.8) - (1.8)^2/2 - 1] = 1 - .98 = .02$

(b) $P(.4 < X < 1.6) = F(1.6) - F(.4) = 2(1.6) - (1.6)^2/2 - 1 - (.4)^2/2 = .84$

5.9 (a) $P(0 \leq \text{error} \leq \pi/4) = \int_0^{\pi/4} \cos x dx = \sin x\big|_0^{\pi/4} = \sin(\pi/4) = \sqrt{2}/2$

(b) $P(\text{phase error} > \pi/3) = \int_{\pi/3}^{\pi/2} \cos x dx = \sin(\pi/2) - \sin(\pi/3) = 1 - \sqrt{3}/2$ $= .1339$

5.13 The density is

$$f(x) = \begin{cases} 4x^3 & 0 < x < 1 \\ 0 & \text{elsewhere} \end{cases}$$

Thus,

$$\mu = \int_0^1 4x^4 dx = 4x^5/5\Big|_0^1 = 4/5$$

$$\mu_2' = \int_0^1 4x^5 dx = 4x^6/6\Big|_0^1 = 2/$$

and the variance is

$$\sigma^2 = \mu_2' - \mu^2 = 2/3 - (4/5)^2 = .0267$$

5.17 The density is:

$$f(x) = \begin{cases} (1/20)e^{-x/20} & x > 0 \\ 0 & x \leq 0 \end{cases}$$

Thus,

$$\mu = \frac{1}{20} \int_0^\infty x e^{-x/20} dx$$

Integrating by parts gives:

$$\mu = -xe^{-x/20}\Big|_0^\infty + \int_0^\infty e^{-x/20} dx = 0 - 20e^{-x/20}\Big|_0^\infty = 20 \text{ (thousand miles)}$$

5.21 (a) $P(X \leq z) = F(z) = .9911$. Thus $z = 2.37$

(b) $P(X > z) = .1093$. Thus $P(X \leq z) = 1 - .1093$ or $F(z) = .8907$. Thus, $z = 1.23$

(c) $P(X > z) = .6443$. Thus, $F(z) = 1 - .6443 = .3557$. Since .3557 is not in Table 3, we use the identity

$$P(X > z) = P(X < -z) = F(-z) = .6443$$

Thus, $-z = .37$ and $z = -.37$

(d) $P(X < z) = 1 - P(X < -z) = 1 - F(-z) = .0217$ Thus, $F(-z) = .9783$. Therefore $z = -2.02$.

(e) $P(-z \leq X \leq z) = .9298$. Thus, $F(z) - F(-z) = .9298$, which implies that $F(z) - 1 + F(z) = .9298$. Thus, $F(z) = (1 + .9298)/2 = .9649$. So, $z = 1.81$

5.25 $P[(X - 6.24)/\sigma > (7.92 - 62.4)/\sigma] = .20$. Thus, $1 - F((79.2 - 62.4)/\sigma) = .20$, and $F((79.2 - 62.4)/\sigma) = .80$. But $F(.845) = .80$. Thus $(79.2 - 62.4)/\sigma = .845$, so $\sigma = 19.88$.

5.33 We need to find μ such that $F((3 - \mu)/.01) = .95$. Thus, from Table 3, $(3 - \mu)/.01 = 1.645$ or $\mu = 2.98355$.

5.37 In this case, $n = 200$, $p = .25$, $\mu = 50$, $\sigma^2 = 37.5$, $\sigma = 6.1237$. Thus,

$$\begin{aligned} P(\text{fewer than 45 fail}) &= F((44.5 - 50)/6.1237) \\ &= F(-.90) = 1 - F(.90) = 1 - .8159 = .1841 \end{aligned}$$

5.41 Let $f(x)$ be the standard normal density. Then $F(-z) = \int_{-\infty}^{-z} f(x)dx$. Using the change of variable, $s = -x$, and the fact that $f(x) = f(-x)$, we have

$$F(-z) = -\int_{\infty}^{z} f(-s)ds = \int_{z}^{\infty} f(s)ds = 1 - \int_{-\infty}^{z} f(s)ds = 1 - F(z)$$

5.45 The uniform density is:

$$f(x) = \begin{cases} 1/(\beta - \alpha) & \alpha < x < \beta \\ 0 & \text{elsewhere} \end{cases}$$

Thus, the distribution function is

$$F(x) = \begin{cases} 1 & x \geq \beta \\ (x - \alpha)/(\beta - \alpha) & \alpha < x < \beta \\ 0 & x \leq \alpha \end{cases}$$

5.49 I_0/I_i is distributed log-normal with $\alpha = 2$, $\beta^2 = .01$, $\beta = .1$. Thus,

$$\begin{aligned} P(7 \leq I_0/I_i \leq 7.5) &= F((\ln(7.5) - 2)/.1) - F((\ln(7) - 2)/.1) \\ &= F(.149) - F(-.54) = F(.149) + F(.54) - 1 \\ &= .5592 - .7054 - 1 = .2646 \end{aligned}$$

5.53 When $\alpha = 2$ and $\beta = 2$, $\Gamma(2) = 1$. So

$$f(x) = \begin{cases} xe^{-x/2}/4 & x > 0 \\ 0 & x \leq 0 \end{cases}$$

Thus,

$$P(X < 4) = \int_0^4 f(x)dx = \frac{1}{4}\int_0^4 xe^{-x/2}dx$$

Integrating by parts gives

$$\begin{aligned} -\frac{1}{2}xe^{-x/2}\,\Big|_0^4 + \frac{1}{2}\int_0^4 e^{-x/2}dx &= 2e^{-2} - e^{-x/2}\,\Big|_0^4 \\ &= 1 - 3e^{-2} = .5940 \end{aligned}$$

5.57 We can ignore the constant in the density since it is always positive. Thus, we need to maximize $f(x) = x^{\alpha-1}e^{-x/\beta}$. Taking the derivative

$$f'(x) = (\alpha-1)x^{\alpha-2}e^{-x/\beta} - x^{\alpha-1}e^{-x/\beta}/\beta = x^{\alpha-2}e^{-x/\beta}(\alpha - 1 - x/\beta)$$

Setting the derivative equal to zero gives the solution $x = \beta(\alpha-1)$. For $\alpha > 1$, the derivative is positive for $x < \beta(\alpha-1)$ and negative for $x > \beta(\alpha-1)$. Thus, $\beta(\alpha-1)$ is a maximum. Note that $x = 0$ is a point of inflection when $\alpha > 2$. When $\alpha = 1$, $f(x) = e^{-x/\beta}$ which has a maximum in the interval $[0,\infty]$ at $x = 0$. When $0 < \alpha < 1$, the derivative does not vanish on $(0,\infty)$ and $f(x)$ is unbounded as x decreases to 0.

5.61 Let N be a random variable having the Poisson distribution with parameter αt. Then $P(N = 0) = (\alpha t)^0 e^{-\alpha t}/0! = e^{-\alpha t}$. Thus, $P(\text{waiting time is} > t) = e^{-\alpha t}$ and $P(\text{waiting time is} < t) = 1 - e^{-\alpha t}$.

5.65 (a) The mean of the beta distribution is given by $\mu = \alpha/(\alpha+\beta)$. Thus, in the case where $\alpha = 1$ and $\beta = 4$, $\mu = 1/(1+4) = 1/5 = .2$

(b) When $\alpha = 1$ and $\beta = 4$, the beta density is

$$\frac{\Gamma(5)}{\Gamma(1)\Gamma(4)}x^0(1-x)^3 = \frac{4!}{0!3!}(1-x)^3 = 4(1-x)^3$$

Thus, the required probability is given by

$$4\int_{.25}^{1}(1-x)^3 dx = -(1-x)^4 \Big|_{.25}^{1} = (.75)^4 = .3164$$

5.69 The probability is

$$\begin{aligned}\int_{4,000}^{\infty}(.025)(.500)x^{-.5}e^{-(.025)x^{.500}}dx &= \int_{\sqrt{4,000}}^{\infty}.025e^{-.025y}dy \\ &= e^{-.025\sqrt{4,000}} = .2057\end{aligned}$$

5.73 (a) $P(X_1 < 1, X_2 < 1) = F(1,1)$

$$= \int_0^1 \int_0^1 x_1 x_2 dx_2 dx_1 = \frac{1}{2} \int_0^1 x_1 dx_1 = \frac{x_1^2}{4} \big|_0^1 = 1/4$$

(b) The probability that the sum is less than 1 is given by:

$$\int_0^1 \int_0^{1-x_1} x_1 x_2 dx_2 dx_1 = (1/2) \int_0^1 x_1(1-x_1)^2 dx_1$$
$$= (1/2)(x_1^4/4 - 2x_1^3/3 + x_1^2/2) \big|_0^1 = (1/2)(1/4 - 2/3 + 1/2) = 1/24$$

5.77 The joint distribution function is given by

$$F(x,y) = \int_0^x \int_0^y \frac{6}{5}(u+v^2) dv du = \frac{3x^2y}{5} + \frac{2xy^3}{5} \quad \text{for } 0 < x < 1,\ 0 < y < 1$$

Thus, the joint distribution is

$$F(x,y) = \begin{cases} 0 & x \le 0 \text{ or } y \le 0 \\ (3/5)x^2y + (2/5)xy^3 & 0 < x < 1,\ 0 < y < 1 \\ (3/5)y + (2/5)y^3 & x \ge 1,\ 0 < y < 1 \\ (3/5)x^2 + (2/5)x & 0 < x < 1,\ y \ge 1 \\ 1 & x \ge 1,\ y \ge 1 \end{cases}$$

The probability of the region in the preceeding exercise is given by

$$\begin{aligned} F(.5,.6) - F(.2,.6) - F(.5,.4) + F(.2,.4) &= .1332 - .03168 - .0728 + .01472 \\ &= .04344 \end{aligned}$$

5.81 (a) To find k, we must integrate the density and set it equal to 1. Thus,

$$\int_0^1 \int_0^2 \int_0^\infty k(x+y)e^{-z} dz dy dx \int_0^1 \int_0^2 k(x+y) dy dx$$

$$= \int_0^1 k(2x+2) dx = 3k = 1$$

Thus, $k = 1/3$.

(b) $P(X < Y,\ Z > 1)$

$$
\begin{aligned}
&= \frac{1}{3}\int_0^1\int_x^2\int_1^\infty (x+y)e^{-z}dzdydx \;=\; \frac{1}{3e}\int_0^1\int_x^2 (x+y)dydx \\
&= \frac{1}{3e}\int_0^1 (2x+2-3x^2/2)dx \;=\; 5/(6e) \;=\; .3066
\end{aligned}
$$

5.85 The expected value of $g(X_1, X_2)$ is

$$
\begin{aligned}
\int_{-\infty}^{\infty} g(x_1,x_2)f(x_1,x_2)dx_1dx_2 &= \int_0^1\int_0^2 (x_1+x_2)x_1x_2dx_2dx_1 \\
&= \int_0^1 (2x_1^2 + 8x_1/3)dx_1 \;=\; 2
\end{aligned}
$$

5.89 (a) $E(X_1 + X_2) = E(X_1) + E(X_2) = 1 + (-1) = 0$.

(b) $Var(X_1 + X_2) = Var(X_1) + Var(X_2) = 5 + 5 = 10$.

5.93 (a) $E(X_1 + X_2 + \cdots + X_{20}) = E(X_1) + E(X_2) + \cdots + E(X_{20})$

$= 20(10) = 200$.

(b) $Var(X_1 + X_2 + \cdots + X_{20}) = Var(X_1) + Var(X_2) + \cdots + Var(X_{20})$

$= 20(3) = 60$.

5.97 (a) The normal-scores plots of the logarithmic, square root and fourth root transformations for the decay time data are given in Figures 5.1, 5.2 and 5.3, respectively.

(b) The normal-scores plots of the logarithmic, square root and fourth root transformations for the interarrival time data are given in Figures 5.4, 5.5 and 5.6, respectively.

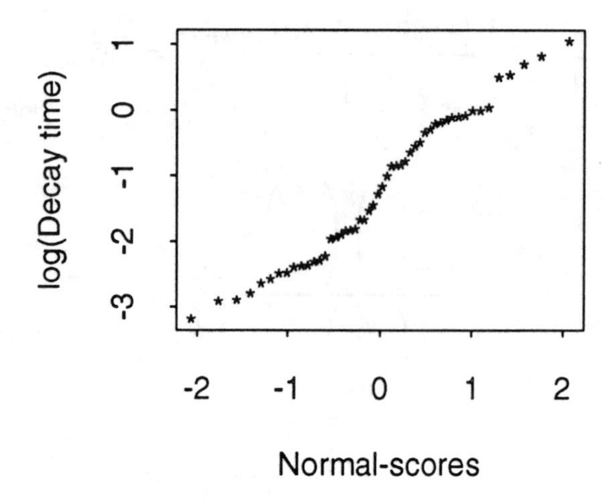

Figure 5.1: Normal-scores plot of the log(decay time) data. Exercise 5.97a

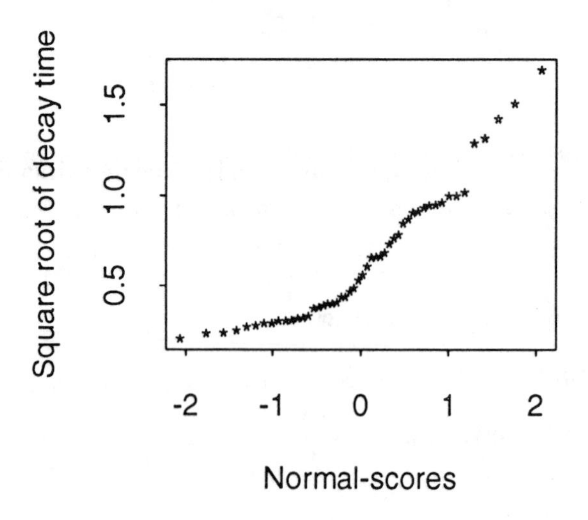

Figure 5.2: Normal-scores plot of square root of the decay time data. Exercise 5.97a

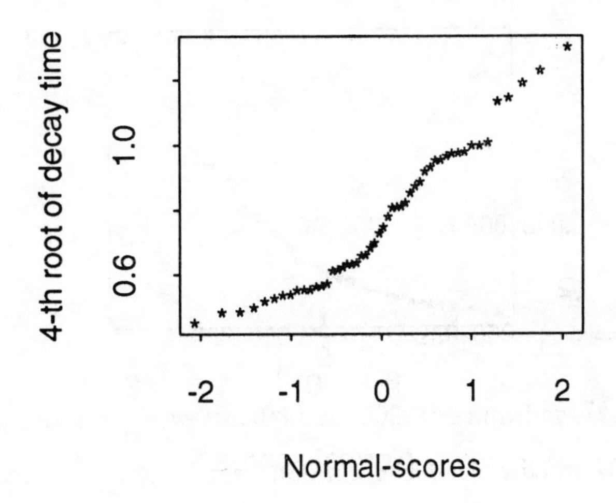

Figure 5.3: Normal-scores plot of fourth root of the decay time data. Exercise 5.97a

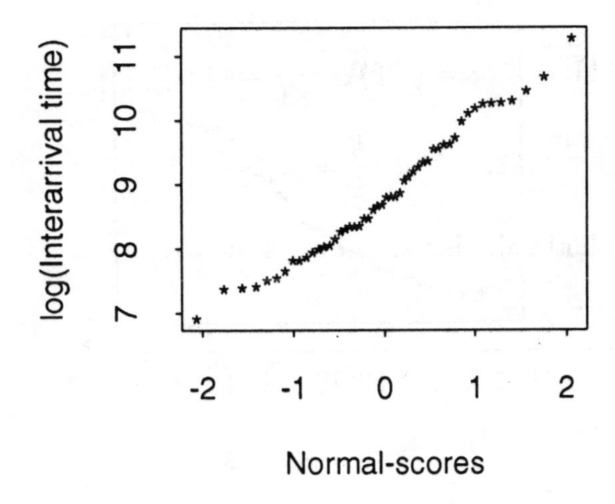

Figure 5.4: Normal-scores plot of the log(interarrival time) data. Exercise 5.97b

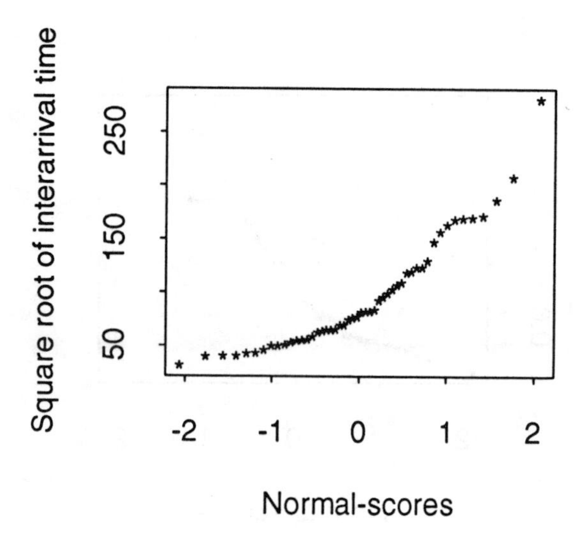

Figure 5.5: Normal-scores plot of square root of the interarrival time data. Exercise 5.97b

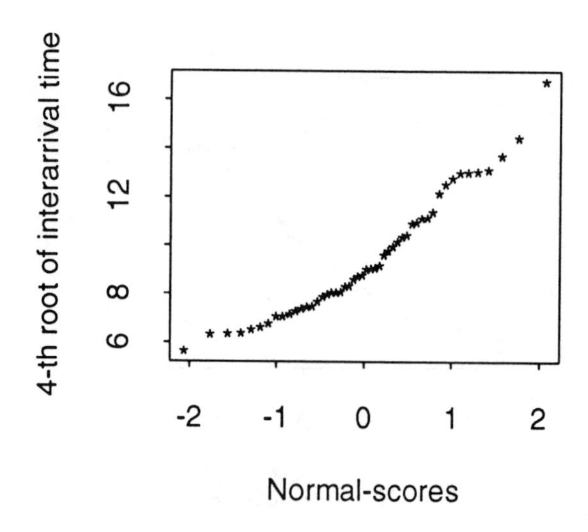

Figure 5.6: Normal-scores plot of fourth root of the interarrival time data. Exercise 5.97b

5.101 (a) The density is

$$f(x) = \begin{cases} .3e^{-.3x} & x > 0 \\ 0 & \text{elsewhere} \end{cases}$$

Thus, the corresponding distribution function is

$$F(x) = \begin{cases} \int_0^x .3e^{-.3s}ds = -e^{-.3s}\mid_0^x = 1 - e^{-.3x} & \text{for } x > 0 \\ 0 & \text{elsewhere} \end{cases}$$

(b) We solve $u = F(x)$ for x. Since $u = F(x) = 1 - e^{-.3x}$, so $e^{-.3x} = 1 - u$ or $-.3x = \ln(1-u)$. The solution is then $x = -\ln(1-u)/.3$

5.105 (a) Histogram of the time of the 100 first failures is

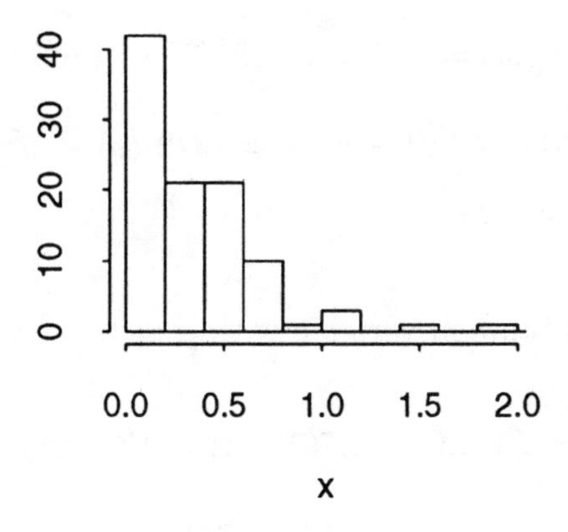

Figure 5.7: Histogram of the 100 first failure times. Exercise 5.105a.

(b) Histogram of the time of the 100 fifth failures is given in Figure 5.8.

5.109 The distribution function is given by:

$$F(x) = \int_{-\infty}^{x} f(s)ds = \int_0^x \frac{3}{2}(1-s^2)ds = \frac{3}{2}(x - x^3/3)$$

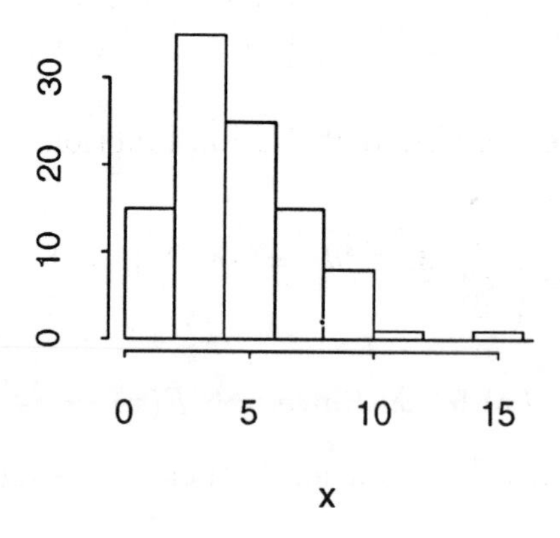

Figure 5.8: Histogram of the 100 fifth failure times. Exercise 5.105b.

Thus,

(a) $P(X < .3) = F(.3) = (3/2)(.3 - .3^3/3) = .4365$

(b) $P(.4 < X < .6) = F(.6) - F(.4) = (3/2)(.6 - .6^3/3) - (3/2)(.4 - .4^3/3)$
$= .792 - .568 = .224.$

5.113 Let X be a normal random variable with $\mu = 4.76$ and $\sigma = .04$

(a) $P(X < 4.66) = F((4.66 - 4.76)/.04) = F(-2.5) = 1 - .9938 = .0062$

(b) $P(X > 4.8) = 1 - F((4.8 - 4.76)/.04) = 1 - F(1) = 1 - .8413 = .1587$

(c) $P(4.7 < X < 4.82) = F(4.82 - 4.76)/.04) - F((4.7 - 4.76)/.04)$
$= 2F(1.5) - 1 = 2(.9332) - 1 = .8664$

5.117 The density function is

$$f(x) = \begin{cases} .25e^{-.25x} & x > 0 \\ 0 & \text{elsewhere} \end{cases}$$

(a) P(time to observe a particle is more than 200 microseconds)

$= -e^{-.25x} \mid_{.2}^{\infty} = e^{-.05} = .951$

(b) P(time to observe a particle is less than 10 microseconds)

$= 1 - e^{-.0025} = 1 - .9975 = .0025$

5.121 Let X be the strength of a support beam, having the Weibull distribution with $\alpha = .02$ and $\beta = 3.0$.

$$P(X > 4.5) = \int_{4.5}^{\infty} (.02)3x^2 e^{-.02x^3}\, dx$$

Using the change of variable $u = x^3$, we have

$$P(X > 4.5) = \int_{(4.5)^3}^{\infty} .02e^{-.02u} du = e^{-.02(4.5)^3} = .1616$$

5.125 (a) $E(X_1 + X_2 + \cdots + X_{30}) = E(X_1) + E(X_2) + \cdots + E(X_{30})$

$= 30(-5) = -150.$

(b) $Var(X_1 + X_2 + \cdots + X_{30}) = Var(X_1) + Var(X_2) + \cdots + Var(X_{30})$

$= 30(2) = 60.$

Chapter 6

SAMPLING DISTRIBUTIONS

6.1 Only if the pieces are put on the assembly line such that every 20-th piece is random with respect to the characteristic being measured.

If twenty molds are dumping their contents, in sequential order, onto the assembly line then the sample would consist of output from a single mold . It would not be random.

6.5 (a) The number of samples (given that order does not matter) is

$$\binom{6}{2} = \frac{6 \cdot 5}{2 \cdot 1} = 15.$$

(b) The number of samples (given that order does not matter) is

$$\binom{25}{2} = \frac{25 \cdot 24}{2 \cdot 1} = 300.$$

6.9 A table of each outcome and the mean follows:

Outcome	Mean	Outcome	Mean
1, 1	1.0	3, 1	2.0
1, 2	1.5	3, 2	2.5
1, 3	2.0	3, 3	3.0
1, 4	2.5	3, 4	3.5
2, 1	1.5	4, 1	2.5
2, 2	2.0	4, 2	3.0
2, 3	2.5	4, 3	3.5
2, 4	3.0	4, 4	4.0

Thus , the distribution of these values is:

Value	No. of Ways Obtained	Probability
1.0	1	.0625
1.5	2	.1250
2.0	3	.1875
2.5	4	.2500
3.0	3	.1875
3.5	2	.1250
4.0	1	.0625

where the probability is (*no. ways*)$\times(.25)^2$. Consequently, the distribution of $\bar{X}$ has mean

$$\mu_{\bar{X}} = 1(.0625) + 1.5(.1250) + \cdots + 3.5(.1250) + 4(.0625) = 2.5$$

which may be obtained directly from the symmetry of the distribution. The distribution of $\bar{X}$ has variance

$$\sigma^2_{\bar{X}} = (1-2.5)^2(.0625) + (1.5-2.5)^2(.1250) + \cdots$$

$$+(3.5-2.5)^2(.1250)+(4-2.5)^2(.0625)$$

$$= .625.$$

Now the mean of the original distribution is also 2.5 and the variance is 1.25. Thus, Theorem 6.1 yields 2.5 and $1.25/2 = .625$ as the mean and the variance of the distribution of the sample mean of two observations. These agree exactly as they must.

6.13 We need to find $P(|\bar{X}-\mu| < .6745 \cdot \sigma/\sqrt{n})$. Since the standard deviation of the mean is $\sigma/\sqrt{n}$, the standardized variable $(\bar{X}-\mu)/(\sigma/\sqrt{n})$ is approximately a normal random variable for large n (central limit theorem). Thus , we need to find:

$$P(|\frac{\bar{X}-\mu}{\sigma/\sqrt{n}}| < .6745).$$

Now, interpolating in Table 3 gives

$$P(\frac{\bar{X}-\mu}{\sigma/\sqrt{n}} < .6745) = .75.$$

Thus,

$$P(\frac{\bar{X}-\mu}{\sigma/\sqrt{n}} \leq -.6745) = P(\frac{\bar{X}-\mu}{\sigma/\sqrt{n}} \geq .6745) = .25$$

so

$$P(|\frac{\bar{X}-\mu}{\sigma/\sqrt{n}}| < .6745) = .75 - .25 = .50.$$

The probability that the mean of a random sample of size n , from a population with standard deviation σ, will differ from μ by less than $(.6745)(\sigma/\sqrt{n})$ is approximately .5 for sufficiently large n.

6.17 We need to find

$$P(\sum_{i=1}^{36} X_i > 6,000) = P(\bar{X} > 166.67) = P(\bar{X} - 163 > 3.67)$$

$$= P(\frac{\bar{X} - 163}{18/6} > 1.222).$$

Since $n = 36$ is relatively large, we use the central limit theorem to approximate this probability by

$$1 - F(-1.222) = .111.$$

6.21 The mean of the data is $\bar{x} = 23$ and the sample standard deviation is 6.39. Thus, if the data is from a normal population with $\mu = 20$, the statistic

$$t = \frac{\bar{x} - \mu}{s/\sqrt{n}} = \frac{23 - 20}{6.39/\sqrt{6}} = 1.15$$

is the value of a t random variable with 5 degrees of freedom. The entry in Table 4 for $\alpha = 10$ and $\nu = 5$ is 1.476. Before the data are observed, we know that

$$P(\frac{\bar{X} - \mu}{S/\sqrt{n}} > 1.15) > .10.$$

Thus, the data does not give strong evidence against the ambulance service's claim.

6.25 We need to find

$$1 - P(\frac{1}{7} \leq \frac{S_1^2}{S_2^2} \leq 7).$$

Since the samples are independent and from normal populations, the statistic S_1^2/S_2^2 has an F distribution with $n_1 - 1 = n_2 - 1 = 7$ degrees of freedom for both the numerator and the denominator. From Table 6(b), we see that

$$P(\frac{S_1^2}{S_2^2} > 6.99) = .01.$$

Using the relation

$$F_{1-\alpha}(\nu_1, \nu_2) = \frac{1}{F_\alpha(\nu_2, \nu_1)},$$

we know that

$$P(\frac{S_1^2}{S_2^2} < \frac{1}{6.99}) = .01.$$

Thus, approximately

$$P(\frac{S_1^2}{S_2^2} < \frac{1}{7} \; or \; \frac{S_1^2}{S_2^2} > 7) = P(\frac{S_1^2}{S_2^2} < \frac{1}{7}) + P(\frac{S_1^2}{S_2^2} > 7) = .01 + .01+ = .02.$$

6.29 The probability that the ratio of the larger to the smaller sample variance exceeds 3 is

$$1 - P(\frac{1}{3} \le \frac{S_1^2}{S_2^2} \le 3) = 1 - \int_{1/3}^{3} \frac{6x}{(1+x)^4}\, dx.$$

Let $u = x + 1$ or $x = u - 1$. Then

$$\begin{aligned} P(\frac{1}{3} \le \frac{S_1^2}{S_2^2} \le 3) &= \int_{4/3}^{4} \frac{6(u-1)}{u^4}\, du = \frac{-3}{u^2} \Big|_{4/3}^{4} + \frac{2}{u^3} \Big|_{4/3}^{4} \\ &= \frac{24}{16} - \frac{52}{64} = .6875. \end{aligned}$$

Thus,

$$1 - P(\frac{1}{3} \le \frac{S_1^2}{S_2^2} \le 3) = 1 - .6875 = .3125.$$

6.33 The finite population correction factor is $(N - n)/(N - 1)$. Thus

(a)

$$\frac{N-n}{N-1} = \frac{8-2}{8-1} = .857.$$

(b)

$$\frac{N-n}{N-1} = \frac{20-2}{20-1} = .947.$$

6.37 By the central limit theorem,

$$\begin{aligned} P(|\bar{X} - \mu| > .06) &= P(\frac{|\bar{X} - \mu|}{\sigma/\sqrt{n}} > \frac{.06}{.16/\sqrt{36}}) \\ &\approx P(|Z| > 2.25) = 2(1 - .9878) = .0244 \end{aligned}$$

6.41 Under this sampling scheme, the observations will not satisfy the independence assumption required for a random sample. The longest lines are likely to occur together when the same cars must wait several light changes during the rush hour.

Chapter 7

INFERENCE CONCERNING MEANS

7.1 (a) There are $\binom{5}{3} = 10$ possible samples of size 3.

Sample	Mean	Probability	Sample	Mean	Probability
3,6,9	6	0.10	3,15,27	15	0.10
3,6,15	8	0.10	6,9,15	10	0.10
3,6,27	12	0.10	6,9,27	14	0.10
3,9,15	9	0.10	6,15,27	16	0.10
3,9,27	13	0.10	9,15,27	17	0.10

(b) We verify that the expected value of $\bar{X}$, for a sample of size 3, is

$$E(\bar{X}) = \frac{1}{10}(6 + 8 + 12 + 9 + 13 + 15 + 10 + 14 + 16 + 17) = \frac{120}{10} = 12.$$

which is equal to the mean of the population. That is, it equals

$$\frac{1}{5}(3 + 6 + 9 + 15 + 27) = \frac{60}{5} = 12$$

7.5 With reference to the Exercise 7.4, the 95 percent confidence interval for the true inter-request time is given by

$$\bar{x} \pm E = 11,795 \pm 3895.57$$

or from 7,899.43 to 15,690.6.

7.9 We need to find $z_{\alpha/2}$ such that

$$10 = z_{\alpha/2} \cdot (62.35)/\sqrt{80}.$$

Thus,

$$z_{\alpha/2} = \sqrt{80} \cdot 10/62.35 = 1.43.$$

From Table 3, we see that F(1.43) = .9236. Thus, $\alpha = 2(1 - .9236) = .1528$. So, the confidence level is about 84.7 percent.

7.13 As discussed in Chapter 6, if a random sample of size n is taken from a population of size N, having mean μ and variance σ^2, then $\bar{X}$ has mean μ and variance $\sigma^2(N-n)/n(N-1)$. Thus, the formula for E becomes

$$E = z_{\alpha/2}\frac{\sigma}{\sqrt{n}} \cdot \sqrt{\frac{N-n}{N-1}}.$$

(a) In this case, $z_{.025} = 1.96$, $s = 85$, $N = 420$, and $n = 50$. Thus,

$$E = 1.96 \cdot \frac{85}{\sqrt{50}}\sqrt{\frac{420-50}{420-1}} = 22.14.$$

Thus, we have 95 percent confidence that the error will be less than 22.14.

(b) In this case, $z_{.005} = 2.575$, $\sigma = 12.2$, $n = 40$, $N = 200$. Thus,

$$E = 2.575\frac{12.2}{\sqrt{40}} \cdot \sqrt{\frac{200-40}{200-1}} = 4.454.$$

Thus, we have 99 percent confidence that the error will be less than 4.454.

7.17 Since the sample size is small, if we can reasonably regard the data as a sample from a normal population, we can use the small sample error bound with $s = 2.48$, $n = 20$, and $t_{.025}$ with 19 degrees of freedom is equal to 2.093. Thus, with 95 percent confidence, we assert that the error is less than

$$\frac{(2.093)(2.48)}{\sqrt{20}} = 1.161$$

7.21 In this case, $t_{.01}$ with 5 degrees of freedom is 3.365. Thus, the 98 percent confidence interval is given by

$$4 - \frac{(3.365)(3.162)}{\sqrt{6}} \quad < \quad \mu \quad < \quad 4 + \frac{(3.365)(3.162)}{\sqrt{6}}$$

or, $-.344 \quad < \quad \mu \quad < \quad 8.344$.

7.25 (a) The probability assigned to the interval 3,500 to 4,000 by the sales manager is given by

$$F\left(\frac{4,000 - 3,800}{260}\right) - F\left(\frac{3,500 - 3,800}{260}\right)$$
$$= F(.769) - F(-1.1538) = F(.769) + F(1.1538) - 1$$
$$= .7791 + .8757 - 1 = .6548$$

(b) Using the formulas in Section 7.3, the posterior normal distribution has mean

$$\mu_1 = \frac{9(3702)(260)^2 + 3800 \cdot (390)^2}{9 \cdot (260)^2 + (390)^2} = 3721.6$$

and,

$$\sigma_1 = \frac{390(260)}{\sqrt{9 \cdot (260)^2 + (390)^2}} = 116.28.$$

Thus, the probability of the interval is given by

$$F\left(\frac{4000-3721.6}{116.28}\right)-F\left(\frac{3500-3721.6}{116.28}\right)$$

$$=F(2.39)-F(-1.906)=.9916+.9716-1=.9632$$

7.29 We can assume from past experience that the standard deviation of the drying times is 2.4 minutes. The null hypothesis is that the mean $\mu = 20$. We reject the null hypothesis if $\bar{X} > 20.50$ minutes.

(a) the probability of a Type I error is the probability that $\bar{X} > 20.50$ when $\mu = 20$. Using a normal approximation to the distribution of the sample mean, this probability is given by

$$1-F\left(\frac{20.50-20}{2.4/\sqrt{36}}\right)=1-F(1.25)=1-.8944=.1056$$

(b) The probability of a Type II error when $\mu = 21$ is the probability that $\bar{X} < 20.50$ when $\mu = 21$. Using a normal approximation to the distribution of the sample mean, this probability is given by

$$F\left(\frac{20.50-20}{2.4/\sqrt{36}}\right)=F(-1.25)=1-F(1.25)=.1056.$$

7.33 (a) The probability of a Type I error is the probability that $\bar{X} < 78.0$ when $\mu = 80.0$. Using the normal approximation to the distribution of the sample mean, this probability is given by

$$F\left(\frac{78.0-80.0}{8.4/\sqrt{100}}\right)=F(-2.38)=.0087$$

(b) The answer is the same since for a composite null hypothesis α is the maximum α for all possible values of the null hypothesis. The maximum occurs when $\mu = 80.0$.

7.37 (a) In this case, use the two-sided alternative $\mu \neq \mu_0$ where μ is the true mean daily inventory under the new marketing policy, and μ_0 is the true mean daily inventory under the old policy (Note: $\mu_0 = 1250$).

(b) The burden of proof is on the new policy. Thus, the alternative is $\mu_0 > \mu$.

(c) The burden of proof is on the old policy. Thus, the alternative is $\mu_0 < \mu$.

7.41 Since the sample is fairly large, we will use the normal approximation to the distribution of the mean substituting s for σ. In this case,

$$z = \frac{1038 - 1000}{146/\sqrt{64}} = 2.08$$

Since we are testing against the one-sided alternative $\mu > 1000$, the critical region is defined by $Z > z_{.05} = 1.645$. Since $2.08 > 1.645$, we reject the null hypothesis.

7.45 We are testing $H_0 : \mu = 14$ against the alternative $H_1 : \mu > 14$ at the .01 level of significance. Since the sample is small, we cannot use the normal approximation. If it is reasonable to assume that the data are from a distribution that is nearly normal, we can use the t statistic. Since the alternative hypothesis is one-sided, the critical region is defined by $t > t_{.01}$ where $t_{.01}$ with 4 degrees of freedom is 3.474. In this case

$$t = \frac{14.9 - 14}{.42/\sqrt{5}} = 4.79$$

Thus, we reject the null hypothesis at the .01 level of significance. The P-value is less than .005 .

7.49 We are testing $H_0 : \mu = 14.0$ against the alternative $H_1 : \mu > 14.0$ at the .05 level of significance. The critical region is defined by $t > t_{.05}$ where $t_{.05}$ with 4 degrees of freedom is 2.132. With the first value changed, $\bar{x} = 14.7$ and

$s = .74162$ so

$$t = \frac{14.7 - 14.0}{.74162/\sqrt{5}} = 2.11.$$

and we cannot reject the null hypothesis. The "paradox" is explained by the standard deviation, which has greatly increased.

7.53 (a) $\mu_0 = 2.000$, $\mu = 2.020$, $\sigma = .050$, $\alpha = .05$, $n = 30$. Thus,

$$d = \frac{|2.020 - 2.000|}{.050} = .4.$$

Since this is a two-sided test, we use Table 8(c). The probability of a Type II error is about .26.

(b) $\mu = 2.030$. Thus,

$$d = \frac{|2.030 - 2.000|}{.050} = .6.$$

The probability of a Type II error is about .15.

(c) $\mu = 2.040$. Thus,

$$d = \frac{|2.040 - 2.000|}{.050} = .8.$$

The probability of a Type II error is about .05.

7.57 Since the alternative is one-sided and $\alpha = .05$, we use Table 8(a) with $n = 8$. The probabilities of a Type II error are about

(a) .59 (b) .32 (c) .12 (d) .03 (e) .00

7.61 (a) Since 21.5 is outside the 95 percent confidence interval, the test in Exercise 7.60 is consistent with the confidence interval.

(b) With the sulfur emission data in C1, the MINITAB output is

```
TINTERVAL 90 PERCENT C1

      N    MEAN   STDEV  SE MEAN    90.0 PERCENT C.I.
C1   80  18.896   5.656    0.632  (  17.843,   19.949)
```

(c) With the aluminum alloy data in C2, the MINITAB output is

```
TINTERVAL 95 C2

         N     MEAN    STDEV  SE MEAN    95.0 PERCENT C.I.
C2      58   70.697    1.797    0.236   (  70.224,   71.169)
```

7.65 Since the samples are fairly large, we use the statistic

$$Z = \frac{(\bar{X}_1 - \bar{X}_2) - \delta}{\sqrt{\sigma_1^2/n_1 + \sigma_2^2/n_2}}$$

The null hypothesis is $\delta = 20$ and the alternative is $\delta \neq 20$. Thus, we reject the null hypothesis if $|Z| > t_{.01/2}$ =2.575. Since

$$z = \frac{292.50 - 266.10}{\sqrt{15.60^2/60 + 18.20^2/60}} = 2.07$$

we cannot reject the null hypothesis. We cannot conclude that the men earn more than twenty dollars per week more than the women.

7.69 In this case, $\bar{X}_c = 58$, $s_c = 109$, $\bar{X}_0 = 51.833$, $s_0 = 160.97$. Since we can assume that the data are from two normal distributions with the same variance, we can use the two-sample t statistic. In this case, we reject the null hypothesis $\mu_1 = \mu_2$ when $|t| > t_{.005}$ with 13 degrees of freedom since the alternative is two-sided. Thus, we reject when $|t| > 3.012$. In this case,

$$t = \frac{58 - 51.833}{\sqrt{8(109) + 5(160.97)}}\sqrt{\frac{9 \cdot 6 \cdot 13}{15}} = 1.03.$$

Thus, we cannot reject the null hypothesis.

7.73 Since $\bar{x}_1 - \bar{x}_2 = .053$ and $n_1 = 32$ and $n_2 = 32$, using the large sample confidence interval with $z_{.025} = 1.96$ gives

$$.053 \pm 1.96\sqrt{\frac{.004^2}{32} + \frac{.005^2}{32}} = .053 \pm .002$$

Hence the 95 percent confidence interval is $.051 < \mu < .055$.

7.77 First, order the cars from 1 to 50. Choose two columns from Table 7. Starting somewhere in the column and going down the page. Select 25 different numbers by discarding 00 and numbers larger than 50. These are the numbered cars in which to install the modified air pollution device.

7.81 The 95 percent confidence interval is given by

$$\bar{x} \pm z_{\alpha/2}\frac{\sigma}{\sqrt{n}} = 26.40 \pm 1.48,$$

so the interval is from 24.92 to 27.88.

7.85 First, we use the error bound from the normal distribution to get an initial estimate of the required sample size. Thus, we need to find n_1 such that

$$\frac{(14,380)(1.96)}{\sqrt{n_1}} = 10,000$$

(since $z_{.025} = 1.96$). Thus, $n_1 = 7.94 \simeq 8$. Now we use $t_{.025} = 2.365$ with 7 degrees of freedom to estimate n_2. Thus n_2 is given by

$$\frac{(14,380)(2.365)}{\sqrt{n_2}} = 10,000$$

or, $n_2 = 11.56 \simeq 12$. Next, we use $t_{.025} = 2.201$ with 11 degrees of freedom to estimate n_3. Thus n_3 is given by

$$\frac{(14,380)(2.201)}{\sqrt{n_3}} = 10,000$$

or, $n_3 = 10.017 \simeq 11$. Now, we use $t_{.025}$ with 10 degrees of freedom to find n_4. Proceeding as before, $n_4 = 10.265 \simeq 11$. Since we have converged to a sample of size 11, 11 observations would be required to have 95 percent confidence that the error is less than 10,000.

7.89 The 90% small sample confidence interval for $\mu_1 - \mu_2$ is

$$(.33 - .25) \pm 1.860\sqrt{\frac{2(.0028) + 6(.0032)}{8}}\sqrt{\frac{10}{3 \cdot 7}}$$

$$= .08 \pm .07 = .01, \ .15$$

7.93 $\mu_0 = 64$, $\mu = 61$, $\sigma = 75$, $\alpha = .05$. Thus, $d = .42$. Since the alternative hypothesis is one-sided, we use Table 8(a) with probability of Type II error .01. The sample size required is about 100.

7.97 (a) Use Table 7 to select 10 cars to install the modified spark plugs. Install the regular plugs to the other cars.

(b) Number the specimens from 1 to 15 and use Table 7 to select 8 numbers between 1 and 20. Use the new oven to bake the specimens having these numbers. Bake the other specimens in the old oven.

Chapter 8

INFERENCES CONCERNING VARIANCES

8.1 (a) The sample variance s^2 is given by

$$s^2 = \frac{1}{n-1}\sum(x_i - \bar{x})^2 = 17.6$$

Thus, the sample standard deviation is $\sqrt{17.6} = 4.195$.

(b) The minimum observation is 21. The maximum observation is 32. thus, the range is 11. Since the sample size is 6, the expected length of the range is 2.534σ. Thus, we estimate σ by $11/2.534 = 4.341$.

8.5 The sample variance is .025. Since the sample size is 5, the $\chi^2_{.01/2}$ with 4 degrees of freedom is 14.860 and $\chi^2_{1-.01/2}$ with 4 degrees of freedom is .207. Thus, if the data are from a normal population, a 99 percent confidence interval for σ^2 is

$$\frac{4(.025)}{14.860} < \sigma^2 < \frac{4(.025)}{.207}$$

or

$$.0067 < \sigma^2 < .483,$$

and the 99 percent confidence interval for the standard deviation is

$$.082 < \sigma < .695$$

8.9 Since the data are from a normal population, we can use the statistic

$$\chi^2 = \frac{(n-1)S^2}{\sigma_0^2}.$$

The null hypothesis is $\sigma = 15.0$ and the alternative is $\sigma > 15.0$. Since the sample size is 71, we reject the null hypothesis if $\chi^2 > \chi^2_{.05}$ with 70 degrees of freedom Thus, we reject the null hypothesis $\sigma = 15.0$ if $\chi^2 > 90.531$. In this case, $s = 19.3$ minutes and the test statistic

$$\chi^2 = \frac{70 \cdot (19.3)^2}{(15.0)^2} = 115.886$$

so we reject the null hypothesis $\sigma = 15.0$ in favor of the alternative $\sigma > 15.0$, at the .05 level of significance.

8.13 Since Exercise 7.67 states that the two samples can be assumed to be from normal populations, we can use the statistic

$$F = \frac{S_M^2}{S_m^2}$$

which has an F distribution with $n_M - 1$ and $n_m - 1$ degrees of freedom. The null hypothesis is $\sigma_1^2 = \sigma_2^2$ and the alternative hypothesis is $\sigma_1^2 \neq \sigma_2^2$. The sample sizes are $n_M = 8$ and $n_m = 10$. Thus, we reject the null hypothesis when $F > F_{.02/2}(7, 9)$ or when $F > 5.61$. In this case $s_M^2 = (1.81)^2$ and $s_m^2 = (1.48)^2$ so

$$F = \left(\frac{1.81}{1.48}\right)^2 = 1.496.$$

Thus, we cannot reject the null hypothesis at the .02 level of significance.

8.17 (a) The two samples are not from normal populations so we cannot directly use a two-sample t test. Also, the population variances may be unequal.

(b) If we take the logarithm of the observations we can test whether or not the means of the transformed data differ by $\log 4$ since the transformed data are samples from two normal populations. However, this does not test whether the means of the original lognormal populations are the ratio 4 to 1 since the sample mean of the transformed data (the mean of the logs) is not the same as the transform of the mean of the data.

8.21 The sample standard deviation is 4.9. The sample size is 25. The null hypothesis is $\sigma^2 = 30.0$ and the alternative is $\sigma^2 < 30.0$. If the data are from a normal population, we can use the statistic

$$\chi^2 = \frac{(n-1)S^2}{\sigma_0^2}.$$

We reject the null hypothesis if $\chi^2 < \chi^2_{1-.05}$ with 24 degrees of freedom or when $\chi^2 < 13.484$. In this case,

$$\chi^2 = \frac{24 \cdot (4.9)^2}{30} = 19.21.$$

Thus, we cannot reject the null hypothesis at the .05 level of significance.

8.25 The variance of the first sample is 7.499 and the sample size is 10. The variance of the second sample is 2.681 and the sample size is 8. The null hypothesis $\sigma_1^2 = \sigma_2^2$ and the alternative hypothesis is $\sigma_1^2 \neq \sigma_2^2$. Assuming normal populations we use the statistic

$$F = \frac{S_M^2}{S_m^2}$$

which has an F distribution with $n_M - 1 = 9$ and $n_m - 1 = 7$ degrees of freedom. The null hypothesis $\sigma_1 = \sigma_2$ will be rejected in favor of the alternative hypothesis $\sigma_1 \neq \sigma_2$ if $F > F_{.01}(9,7) = 6.72$. In this case

$$F = \frac{7.499}{2.681} = 2.797$$

so we cannot reject the null hypothesis at the .02 level of significance.

Chapter 9

INFERENCES CONCERNING PROPORTIONS

9.1 (a) The sample proportion is .42. Using Table 9(a) for sample size 200 gives the 95% confidence interval for p,

$$.35 < p < .49.$$

(b) The large sample 95% confidence interval for p obtained by substituting $x/n = .42$ and $z_{\alpha/2} = 1.96$ is

$$.42 - 1.96\sqrt{\frac{(.42)(.58)}{200}} < p < .42 + 1.96\sqrt{\frac{(.42)(.58)}{200}}$$

or

$$.352 < p < .488.$$

9.5 (a) The sample proportion is .38. Using Table 9(a) and interpolating between sample sizes 200 and 400 gives

$$.315 + (.33 - .315)/4 < p < .45 - (.45 - .43)/4$$

or

$$.319 < p < .445.$$

(b) Using the large sample formula for the maximum error with $x/n = .38$ and $z_{\alpha/2}$ =1.96 gives

$$E = 1.96\sqrt{\frac{(.38)(.62)}{250}} = .06.$$

Thus, the error is bounded by .06 with 95% confidence.

9.13 Using the formula for 'known' p with $p = .4$, $z_{\alpha/2} = 2.575$, and $E = .035$ gives

$$n = (.4)(.6)\left(\frac{2.575}{.035}\right)^2 = 1299.06.$$

The required sample size is 1300.

9.17 Since in this case p is small, we use the upper confidence limit derived from the Poisson approximation. Here $n = 500$, the number of degrees of freedom is $2(7+1) = 16$, and $\chi^2_{.05}$ with 16 degrees of freedom is 26.296. Thus, the 95% upper confidence bound is

$$p < \frac{1}{(2)(500)} \cdot 26.296 = .026.$$

9.21 The mean and variance of a beta distribution with parameters α and β are:

$$\mu = \frac{\alpha}{\alpha+\beta}, \qquad \sigma^2 = \frac{\alpha\beta}{(\alpha+\beta)^2(\alpha+\beta+1)}.$$

In this case $\mu = .20$ and $\sigma^2 = (.0125)^2$. Solving for α and β gives:

$$\alpha \;=\; \mu\left(\frac{(1-\mu)\mu}{\sigma^2} - 1\right) = 204.6,$$

$$\beta = (1-\mu)\left(\frac{(1-\mu)\mu}{\sigma^2} - 1\right) = 818.4.$$

The posterior distribution is beta with parameters $x+\alpha$ and $n-x+\beta$ if x defectives were observed. In this case, $x = 86$ and $n = 200$, so the new parameters are

$$\alpha_1 = 86 + 204.6 = 290.6,$$

and

$$\beta_1 = 200 - 86 + 818.4 = 932.4.$$

Thus, the mean of the posterior distribution is

$$\mu = \frac{290.6}{290.6 + 932.4} = .238.$$

9.25 The null hypothesis is $p = .40$. The alternative is $p < .40$. Thus we reject the null hypothesis when the large sample statistic Z is such that $Z < -z_{.01} = -2.33$. In this case,

$$Z = \frac{49 - 150(.40)}{\sqrt{150(.40)(.60)}} = -1.83.$$

Thus, we cannot reject the the service's claim.

9.29 The null hypothesis is $p = .50$, the alternative is $p \neq .50$, and the significance level is .05. Proceeding in a similar fashion to the preceding problem, we reject the null hypothesis if $X \leq 3$ or $X \geq 12$. The actual level of significance would be

$$P[\, X \leq 3 \text{ or } X \geq 12 \mid n = 15, p = .50 \,] = .0176 + (1 - .9824) = .0352.$$

9.33 We use the χ^2 statistic with 2 degrees of freedom to test the null hypothesis that the actual proportions are the same against the alternative that they are not the same. Thus, we reject the null hypothesis at the 1% level when $\chi^2 >$

$\chi^2_{.01} = 9.210$. In Table 9.3, the expected frequency and the contribution to the χ^2 statistic of each cell are given in the parentheses and brackets respectively.

Table 9.3. Exercise 9.33.

	Agency I	Agency II	Agency III	Total
For the pension plan	67 (65.00) [.06]	84 (97.50) [1.87]	109 (97.50) [1.36]	260
Against the pension plan	33 (35.00) [.11]	66 (52.50) [3.47]	41 (52.50) [2.52]	140
Total	100	150	150	400

The χ^2 statistic is

$$\begin{aligned}\chi^2 &= \frac{2.00^2}{65.00} + \frac{13.50^2}{97.50} + \frac{11.50^2}{97.50} + \\ &\quad \frac{2.00^2}{35.00} + \frac{13.50^2}{52.50} + \frac{11.50^2}{52.50} = 9.39.\end{aligned}$$

Thus, we reject the null hypothesis.

9.37 Let p_1 and p_2 be proportions of reworking units before and after the training respectively. The 99% confidence interval for the true difference of the proportions, $p_1 - p_2$, is

$$x_1/n_1 - x_2/n_2 \pm z_{\alpha/2}\sqrt{\frac{(x_1/n_1)(1 - x_1/n_1)}{n_1} + \frac{(x_2/n_2)(1 - x_2/n_2)}{n_2}}$$

$$= 26/200 - 12/200 \pm 2.575\sqrt{\frac{(26/200)(1 - 26/200)}{200} + \frac{(12/200)(1 - 12/200)}{200}}$$

$$= .07 \pm .075$$

or

$$-.005 < p_1 - p_2 < .145.$$

9.41 Notice that $n = \sum_j n_j$ and

$$e_{1j} = n_j \frac{x}{n}, \qquad e_{2j} = n_j \frac{n-x}{n}.$$

The sum of the expected frequencies of the first row is

$$\sum_j e_{1j} = \sum_j n_j \frac{x}{n} = \frac{x}{n} \sum_j n_j = x.$$

Similarly, the sum of the expected frequencies of the second row is

$$\sum_j e_{2j} = \sum_j n_j \frac{n-x}{n} = \frac{n-x}{n} \sum_j n_j = n-x.$$

Also, the sum of the expected frequencies of the jth column is

$$e_{1j} + e_{2j} = n_j \frac{x}{n} + n_j \frac{n-x}{n} = n_j.$$

9.45 To test the null hypothesis that there is no dependence between fidelity and selectivity against the alternative that there is dependence at the 1% level, we use the χ^2 statistic with 4 degrees of freedom and reject the null hypothesis when $\chi^2 > \chi^2_{.01} = 13.277$. In Table 9.7, the expected frequency and the contribution to the χ^2 statistic of each cell are given in the parentheses and brackets respectively.

Table 9.7. Exercise 9.45.

Selectivity		Fidelity: Low	Average	High	Total
	Low	6 (13.68) [4.31]	12 (23.16) [5.38]	32 (13.16) [26.98]	50
	Average	33 (30.65) [.18]	61 (51.87) [1.61]	18 (29.47) [4.47]	112
	High	13 (7.66) [3.72]	15 (12.97) [.32]	0 (7.37) [7.37]	28
	Total	52	88	50	190

The χ^2 statistic is

$$\begin{aligned}\chi^2 &= \frac{7.68^2}{13.68} + \frac{11.16^2}{23.16} + \frac{18.84^2}{13.16} + \\ &\quad \frac{2.35^2}{30.65} + \frac{9.13^2}{51.87} + \frac{11.47^2}{29.47} + \\ &\quad \frac{5.34^2}{7.66} + \frac{2.03^2}{12.97} + \frac{7.37^2}{7.37} \\ &= 54.328.\end{aligned}$$

Thus, we reject the null hypothesis and conclude that there is dependence between fidelity and selectivity. The major contributions to χ^2 come from the High Fidelity categories. The Low Selectivity-High Fidelity count is very high.

9.49 The mean of the distribution is 2.0. Using Table 9.10 to obtain the Poisson probabilities for $\lambda = 2.0$, the expected frequencies are:

Table 9.10. Exercise 9.49.

Number	Frequency		Poisson prob. λ=2.0	Expected frequency	
0	52		.135	67.5	
1	151		.271	135.5	
2	130		.271	135.5	
3	102		.180	90.0	
4	45		.090	45.0	
5	12		.036	18.0	
6	5		.012	6.0	
7	1	} 8	.004	2.0	} 8.5
8	2		.001	.5	

We use the χ^2 statistic with $7 - 2 = 5$ degrees of freedom to test the null hypothesis that the arrival distribution is Poisson. Thus, we reject the null hypothesis at the 5% level when $\chi^2 > \chi^2_{.05} = 11.070$. Now,

$$\chi^2 = \frac{(52-67.5)^2}{67.5} + \frac{(151-135.5)^2}{135.5} + \frac{(130-135.5)^2}{135.5} + \frac{(102-90.0)^2}{90.0} + \frac{(45-45.0)^2}{45.0} + \frac{(12-18.0)^2}{18.0} + \frac{(8-8.5)^2}{8.5} = 9.185.$$

Thus, we cannot reject the null hypothesis.

9.53 We reject the null hypothesis if $\chi^2 > \chi^2_{.05} = 5.991$ for $3 - 1 = 2$ degrees of freedom. The MINITAB commands and output are:

```
NAME C1 'Method 1' C2 'Method 2' C3 'Method 3'
READ C1-C3
31 42 22
19  8 28
```

```
END

CHISQUARE C1-C3


Expected counts are printed below observed counts


       Method 1 Method 2 Method 3    Total
    1        31       42       22       95
          31.67    31.67    31.67


    2        19        8       28       55
          18.33    18.33    18.33


Total        50       50       50      150


ChiSq =  0.014 +  3.372 +  2.951 +
         0.024 +  5.824 +  5.097 = 17.282
df = 2
```

9.57 (a) The sample proportion is $24/160 = .15$. Using Table 9(b) and interpolating between sample sizes 100 and 200 gives

$$.075 + (3/5)(.09 - .075) < p < .225 + (2/5)(.27 - .225)$$

or

$$.084 < p < .243.$$

(b) Using the large sample confidence interval with $x/n = .15$ and $z_{\alpha/2} = 2.575$

gives the 99% confidence interval

$$.15 - 2.575\sqrt{\frac{(.15)(.85)}{160}} < p < .15 + 2.575\sqrt{\frac{(.15)(.85)}{160}}$$

or

$$.077 < p < .223.$$

9.61 Since p is small, we use the upper confidence limit derived from the Poisson approximation. Here n = 4,000, the number of degrees of freedom is 2(10+1) = 22, and $\chi^2_{.05}$ with 22 degrees of freedom is 33.924. Thus, the 95% upper confidence bound is

$$p < \frac{1}{(2)(4,000)} \cdot 33.924 = .0042.$$

9.65 We use the Z statistic in Section 9.4. The null hypothesis is $p_A = p_B$ and the alternative is $p_A < p_B$. Thus, we reject the null hypothesis at the .05 level when $Z < -1.645$. In this case,

$$\hat{p} = \frac{11 + 19}{50 + 50} = .30,$$

and

$$Z = \frac{11/50 - 19/50}{\sqrt{(.30)(.70)(1/50 \ + \ 1/50)}} = -1.746.$$

Consequently, we reject the null hypothesis and conclude that agent A is better than agent B.

9.69 The data are summarized in the table:

Table 9.17. Exercise 9.69.

Number of failures	Number of days	Poisson prob. for $\lambda = 3.2$	Expected frequency
0	9	.041	12.3
1	43	.130	39.0
2	64	.209	62.7
3	62	.223	66.9
4	42	.178	53.4
5	36	.114	34.2
6	22	.060	18.0
7	14	.028	8.4
8	6 } 8	.011	3.3 } 5.1
9	2	.004	1.2
$\geq$ 10	0	.002	.6

We use the χ^2 statistic with $9 - 1 = 8$ degrees of freedom to test the null hypothesis that the data are from a Poisson distribution with $\lambda = 3.2$. We reject the null hypothesis at the 5% level when $\chi^2 > \chi^2_{.05} = 15.507$. In this case,

$$\begin{aligned}\chi^2 &= \frac{3.3^2}{12.3} + \frac{4.0^2}{39.0} + \frac{1.3^2}{62.7} + \\ &\quad \frac{4.9^2}{66.9} + \frac{11.4^2}{53.4} + \frac{1.8^2}{34.2} + \\ &\quad \frac{4.0^2}{18.0} + \frac{5.6^2}{8.4} + \frac{2.9^2}{5.1} \\ &= 10.481.\end{aligned}$$

Thus, we cannot reject the null hypothesis.

Chapter 10

NONPARAMETRIC STATISTICS

10.1

1. *Null hypothesis:* $\tilde{\mu} = 0.55$ $(p = \frac{1}{2})$

   Alternative hypothesis: $\tilde{\mu} \neq 0.55$ $(p > \frac{1}{2})$

2. *Level of significance:* $\alpha = 0.05$.

3. *Criterion:* The criterion may be based on the number of plus signs or the number of minus signs. Using the number of plus signs, denoted by x, reject the null hypothesis if either the probability of getting x or more plus signs or the probability of getting x or fewer plus signs is less than or equal to 0.05/2.

4. *Calculations:* The signs of the differences between the observations and $\tilde{\mu} = .55$ are:

   $$+ \; + \; - \; 0 \; + \; 0 \; - \; + \; + \; - \; + \; + \; - \; + \; + \; - \; + \; -$$

   Ignoring the two 0's, for the cases where the values equal 0.55, we have x =10 and the effective sample size is n =16. From the binomial distribution, Table 1, the probability of $X \geq 10$ with $p = 0.5$ is $1 - .7728 = .2272$. The probability of $X \leq 10$ is .8949.

5. *Decision:* Since both of the probabilities are greater than $0.05/2 = .025$,

we fail to reject the null hypothesis $\tilde{\mu} = 0.55$, at the level $\alpha = .05$.

10.5

1. *Null hypothesis:* $\tilde{\mu} = 6.5$ $(p = \frac{1}{2})$

   Alternative hypothesis: $\tilde{\mu} < 6.5$ $(p < \frac{1}{2})$

2. *Level of significance:* $\alpha = 0.01$.

3. *Criterion:* The criterion may be based on the number of plus signs or the number of minus signs. Using the number of plus signs, denoted by x, reject the null hypothesis if the probability of getting x or fewer positives is less than or equal to 0.01. Using the normal approximation, we reject H_0 if

$$z = \frac{x + .5 - n/2}{\sqrt{n(1/2)(1/2)}} < -2.327$$

4. *Calculations:* The signs of the differences between the observations and $\tilde{\mu} = 150$ are:

$$- \; - \; - \; - \; - \; - \; - \; - \; - \; - \; - \; - \; - \; - \; - \; - \; - \; - \; - \; -$$

$$+ \; - \; - \; - \; + \; - \; + \; + \; - \; - \; - \; + \; - \; + \; - \; - \; + \; + \; - \; -$$

$$+ \; + \; - \; + \; - \; - \; - \; - \; + \; - \; - \; + \; + \; + \; + \; - \; - \; - \; - \; -$$

$$- \; - \; - \; - \; - \; - \; + \; - \; + \; - \; - \; - \; - \; - \; + \; - \; + \; - \; + \; +$$

The sample size is $n = 80$ and we have $x = 22$ positives. Using the normal approximation to the binomial with $p = 0.5$,

$$z = \frac{22.5 - 80/2}{\sqrt{80(1/2)(1 - 1/2)}} = -3.91$$

5. *Decision:* Since $z = -3.91$, we reject the null hypothesis in favor of $\tilde{\mu} < 6.5$, at the level $\alpha = .01$.

10.9 1. *Null hypothesis:* Populations are identical.

Alternative hypothesis: Populations are not identical.

2. *Level of significance:* $\alpha = 0.05$.

3. *Criterion:* We reject the null hypothesis if U_1 is too small or too large. That is, we reject H_0 if

$$Z = \frac{U_1 - \mu_{U_1}}{\sigma_{U_1}} < -1.96 \quad or \quad Z > 1.96.$$

4. *Calculations:* The ranks for the first sample are

$$3, 25, 6, 223, 14, 20, 19, 11, 27, 16, 5, 10, 9, 2, 18$$

and the sum of ranks of the first sample is $W_1 = 208$. Then,

$$U_1 = W_1 - \frac{n_1(n_1+1)}{2} = 208 - \frac{15 \cdot 16}{2} = 88.$$

Under the null hypothesis, the mean and variance of the U_1 statistic are

$$\mu_{U_1} = \frac{n_1 \cdot n_2}{2} = \frac{15 \cdot 12}{2} = 90.$$

and

$$\sigma^2_{U_1} = \frac{n_1 \cdot n_2(n_1 + n_2 + 1)}{12} = \frac{15 \cdot 12(15 + 12 + 1)}{12} = 420.$$

Thus, the Z statistic is

$$Z = \frac{88 - 90}{\sqrt{420}} = -0.0976$$

5. *Decision:* We cannot reject the null hypothesis at the .05 level of significance.

10.13 1. *Null hypothesis:* Populations are identical.

Alternative hypothesis: The first population is stochastically larger than the second.

2. *Level of significance:* $\alpha = 0.05$.

3. *Criterion:* We reject the null hypothesis if U_1 is too large. That is, we reject H_0 if

$$Z = \frac{U_1 - \mu_{U_1}}{\sigma_{U_1}} > 1.645$$

4. *Calculations:* The ranks for the first sample are

$$3, 20, 32, 25, 11.5, 14, 24, 27.5, 17.5, 21, 1, 22, 29, 10, 19, 30.5$$

The sum of ranks of the first sample is

$$W_1 = 307$$

Thus,

$$U_1 = W_1 - \frac{n_1(n_1+1)}{2} = 307 - \frac{16 \cdot 17}{2} = 171.$$

Under the null hypothesis, the mean and variance of the U_1 statistic are

$$\mu_{U_1} = \frac{n_1 \cdot n_2}{2} = \frac{16 \cdot 16}{2} = 128$$

and

$$\sigma^2_{U_1} = \frac{n_1 \cdot n_2(n_1 + n_2 + 1)}{12} = \frac{16 \cdot 16(16 + 16 + 1)}{12} = 704.$$

Thus, the Z statistic is

$$Z = \frac{171 - 120}{\sqrt{704}} = 1.621$$

5. *Decision:* We cannot reject the null hypothesis at the .05 level of significance. In other words , we cannot conclude that strength of material 1 is

stochastically larger than that of material 2.

10.17 1. *Null hypothesis:* Arrangement is random.

Alternative hypothesis: Arrangement is not random.

2. *Level of significance:* $\alpha = 0.05$.

3. *Criterion:* We reject the null hypothesis if

$$Z = \frac{u - \mu_u}{\sigma_u} < -1.96 \quad or \quad Z > 1.96.$$

where u is the total number of runs and

$$\mu_u = \frac{2n_1n_2}{n_1 + n_2} + 1$$

and

$$\sigma_u^2 = \frac{2n_1n_2(2n_1n_2 - n_1 - n_2)}{(n_1 + n_2)^2(n_1 + n_2 - 1)}$$

4. *Calculations:* The runs in the data are underlined.

$$\underline{LL}\ \underline{O}\ \underline{LLLL}\ \underline{OO}\ \underline{LLLL}\ \underline{O}\ \underline{L}\ \underline{OO}\ \underline{LLLL}\ \underline{O}\ \underline{L}\ \underline{OO}\ \underline{LLLLL}$$

$$\underline{O}\ \underline{LLL}\ \underline{OL}\ \underline{O}\ \underline{LLLL}\ \underline{OO}\ \underline{L}\ \underline{OOOO}\ \underline{LLLL}\ \underline{O}\ \underline{L}\ \underline{OO}\ \underline{LLL}\ \underline{O}$$

There are $u = 28$ runs, 22 O's and 38 L's. Under the null hypothesis, the mean and standard deviation are

$$\begin{aligned}
\mu_u &= \frac{2n_1n_2}{n_1 + n_2} + 1 = \frac{2 \cdot 22 \cdot 38}{22 + 38} + 1 = 28.87 \\
\sigma_u &= \sqrt{\frac{2n_1n_2(2n_1n_2 - n_1 - n_2)}{(n_1 + n_2)^2(n_1 + n_2 - 1)}} \\
&= \sqrt{\frac{2 \cdot 22 \cdot 38(2 \cdot 22 \cdot 38 - 22 - 38)}{(22 + 38)^2(22 + 38 - 1)}} = 3.562
\end{aligned}$$

Thus, the Z statistic is

$$Z = \frac{28 - 28.87}{3.562} = -.244$$

5. *Decision:* We cannot reject the null hypothesis at the .05 level of significance.

10.21

1. *Null hypothesis:* The arrangement of sample values is random.
   Alternative hypothesis: The arrangement is not random.
2. *Level of significance:* $\alpha = 0.05$.
3. *Criterion:* We reject the null hypothesis if

$$Z = \frac{u - \mu_u}{\sigma_u} < -1.96 \quad or \quad Z > 1.96.$$

   where u is the total number of runs above and below the median.

4. *Calculations:* The median of the data is 36. Using a for observations above the median and b for those below, the data are:

$$\underline{bbbbbb}\ \underline{a}\ \underline{bbbbbbb}\ \underline{aa}\ \underline{bbbbbbb}\ \underline{aaa}\ \underline{bbb}\ \underline{aa}\ \ \underline{b}\ \underline{aaaaa}\ \underline{b}\ \underline{aaaaaaaaaaa}$$

   There are $u = 12$ runs, 25 a's and 25 b's. In this case

$$\mu_u = \frac{2 \cdot 25 \cdot 25}{25 + 25} + 1 = 26$$

   and

$$\sigma_u = \sqrt{\frac{2 \cdot 25 \cdot 25(2 \cdot 25 \cdot 25 - 25 - 25}{25 + 25)^2(25 + 25 - 1)}} = 3.448$$

   so

$$Z = \frac{12 - 26}{3.449} = -4.005$$

5. *Decision:* We reject the null hypothesis. at the .05 level of significance.

The P- value is .00006.

10.25 1. *Null hypothesis:* $\tilde{\mu} = 0 (p = \frac{1}{2})$

Alternative hypothesis: $\tilde{\mu} > 0$ $(p > \frac{1}{2})$

2. *Level of significance:* $\alpha = 0.063$.

3. *Criterion:* The criterion may be based on the number of plus signs or the number of minus signs. Using the number of plus signs, denoted by x, reject the null hypothesis if the probability of getting x or more positives is less than or equal to 0.063.

4. *Calculations:* The signs of the differences are:

$$+ + - + + + + +$$

The sample size is $n = 7$ and we have $x = 6$ positives. From the binomial distribution, Table 1, the probability of $X \geq 6$, when $p = .5$, is $1 - .9357 = .0625$.

5. *Decision:* Since the probability .0625 is less than .063 we reject the null hypothesis.

10.29 1. *Null hypothesis:* The three populations are identical.

Alternative hypothesis: Populations are not all equal.

2. *Level of significance:* $\alpha = 0.05$.

3. *Criterion:* We reject the null hypothesis if $H > 5.991$ the value of $\chi^2_{.05}$ for 2 degrees of freedom.

4. *Calculations:* The sums of ranks for the samples are

$$R_1 = 1.5 + 5 + 7.5 + 10.5 + 12 + 13 + 15.5 + 18 + 25 + 28 = 136$$

$$R_2 = 3 + 5 + 7.5 + 9 + 10.5 + 20 + 21 + 22.5 + 28 + 30 = 156.5$$

$$R_3 = 1.5 + 5 + 14 + 15.5 + 18 + 18 + 22.5 + 25 + 25 + 28 = 172.5$$

Thus ,

$$H = \frac{12}{30 \cdot 31}[\frac{(136)^2}{10} + \frac{(156.5)^2}{10} + \frac{(172.5)^2}{10}] - 3 \cdot 31 = 0.904.$$

5. *Decision:* We cannot reject the null hypothesis at the .05 level of significance.

10.33 1. *Null hypothesis:* Populations are identical.

Alternative hypothesis: The Heat 1 population is stochastically larger than the Heat 2 population.

2. *Level of significance:* $\alpha = 0.033$.

3. *Criterion:* We reject the null hypothesis if U_1 is too large. Since the distribution of U_1 is symmetric about $n_1 n_2/2 = 10.5$, $.033 = P(U_1 \le 2) = P(U_1 \ge 19)$ and we reject H_0 if $U_1 \ge 19$.

4. *Calculations:* The sum of ranks of the first sample is

$$W_1 = 6 + 9 + 10 = 25$$

Thus,

$$U_1 = W_1 - \frac{n_1(n_1+1)}{2} = 25 - \frac{3 \cdot 4}{2} = 19.$$

5. *Decision:* We reject the null hypothesis at the .033 level of significance and conclude that the Method B population is stochastically larger than the Method A population.

Chapter 11

CURVE FITTING

11.1 (a) The hand-drawn line in the scattergram yields a prediction of 67 percent for the extraction efficiency when the extraction time is 35 minutes.

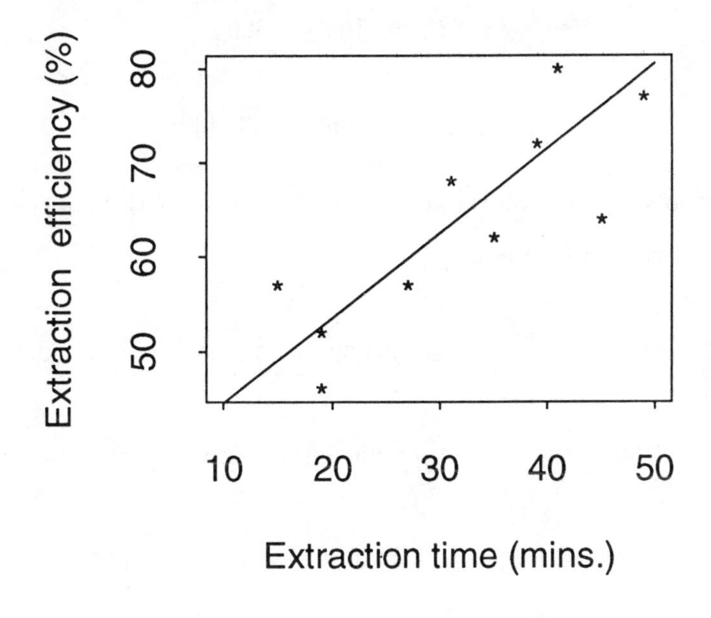

Figure 11.1: Scattergram for Exercise 11.1.

(b) The normal equations are

$$\sum_{i=1}^{n} y_i = a \cdot n + b \sum_{i=1}^{n} x_i$$

$$\sum_{i=1}^{n} x_i y_i = a \sum_{i=1}^{n} x_i + b \sum_{i=1}^{n} x_i^2$$

In this example, n=10

$$\sum_{i=1}^{n} y_i = 635, \quad \sum_{i=1}^{n} x_i = 320$$

$$\sum_{i=1}^{n} x_i^2 = 11,490, \quad \sum_{i=1}^{n} x_i y_i = 21,275$$

So, the system of equations

$$635 = 10a + 320b$$

$$21,275 = 320a + 11,490b$$

must be solved. The solution is a =39.052 and b=.764. Thus, the equation for the least squares line is:

$$y = 39.052 + .764x$$

The prediction of the extraction efficiency when the extraction time is 35 minutes is

$$39.052 + (.764)(35) = 65.79 \text{ percent}$$

11.5 The limits of prediction at x_0 are

$$a + bx_0 \pm t_{\frac{\alpha}{2}}\, s_e \sqrt{1 + \frac{1}{n} + \frac{(x_0 - \bar{x})^2}{S_{xx}}}$$

For Example 11.3, when the tensile force is 3.5 thousand pounds, this becomes

$$51.84 \pm 2.776 \sqrt{15.676} \sqrt{1 + \frac{1}{6} + \frac{(3.5 - 3.5)^2}{17.5}}$$

Thus, the interval is from 39.97 to 63.71 thousandths of an inch.

11.9 (a) We calculate

	x	y	$x - \bar{x}$	$y - \bar{y}$	$(x - \bar{x})(y - \bar{y})$	$(x - \bar{x})^2$	$(y - \bar{y})^2$
	1	2	−2	−4	8	4	16
	2	5	−1	−1	1	1	1
	3	4	0	−2	0	0	4
	4	9	1	3	3	1	9
	5	10	2	4	8	4	16
Total	15	30	0	0	20	10	46

So $S_{xx} = 10$, $S_{yy} = 46$ and $S_{xy} = 20$. Also, $\bar{x} = 3$ and $\bar{y} = 6$. Thus,

$$b = \frac{100}{50} = 2$$
$$a = 6 - (2)(3) = 0$$

So, the least squares line is

$$\hat{y} = 0 + 2x$$

(b) When $x = 3.5$, the prediction is

$$\hat{y} = 2(3.5) = 7$$

11.13 This calculation is the same as in 11.12b except that 1 is added under the square root and t is now $t_{.025}$ with 10 degrees of freedom. Thus, the interval for prediction is given by

$$9.812 \pm 2.228\ (1.101)\ \sqrt{1 + \frac{1}{12} + \frac{(40 - 44.4)^2}{854.9167}}$$

So the interval for the moisture content prediction is from 7.232 to 12.392.

11.17 (a) We wish to minimize

$$\begin{aligned}\sum_{i=1}^{n}(y_i - \beta x_i)^2 &= \sum_{i=1}^{n}(y_i - bx_i + bx_i - \beta x_i)^2 \\ &= \sum_{i=1}^{n}(y_i - bx_i)^2 + (b-\beta)^2\sum_{i=1}^{n}x_i^2 + 2(\beta - b)\sum_{i=1}^{n}(y_i - bx_i)x_i \\ &= \sum_{i=1}^{n}(y_i - bx_i)^2 + (b-\beta)^2\sum_{i=1}^{n}x_i^2 \ + \ 0\end{aligned}$$

by the definition of b. The first term does not depend on β and the second is a minimum for $\beta = b$, thus establishing the result.

(b) In Exercise 11.3, $\sum_{i=1}^{n} y_i x_i = 1342$ and $\sum_{i=1}^{n} x_i^2 = 91$, so that $b = 1342/91 = 14.747$. The previous slope estimate was 14.486. This estimate (14.747) is a little larger.

(c) In Exercise 11.14, $\sum_{i=1}^{n} y_i x_i = 6217$ and $\sum_{i=1}^{n} x_i^2 = 244$, so that $b = 6217/244 = 25.4795$. The previous slope estimate was 24.93. This estimate (25.4795) is a little larger again.

11.21 (a) Instead of $x = (1, 2, 3, 4, 5, 6, 7)$, we will use $x = (-3, -2, -1, 0, 1, 2, 3)$. Then, $\bar{x} = 0$. Thus,

$$a = \sum_{i=1}^{n} y_i/n \quad \text{and} \quad b = \sum_{i=1}^{n} x_i y_i / \sum_{i=1}^{n} x_i^2$$

Since, $\sum_{i=1}^{n} y_i = 23.7$, $\sum_{i=1}^{n} x_i y_i = 19$, $\sum_{i=1}^{n} x_i^2 = 28$,

$$a = 23.7/7 = 3.386 \quad \text{and} \quad b = .679$$

Thus, the least squares line is $\hat{y} = 3.386 + .649x$. The 8'th year corresponds to $x = 4$, so the prediction is

$$3.386 + .679(4) = 6.102.$$

(b) We use $x = (-7, -5, -3, -1, 1, 3, 5, 7)$. Thus, $\sum_{i=1}^{n} y_i = 23.6$, $\sum_{i=1}^{n} x_i y_i = 40.6$, $\sum_{i=1}^{n} x_i^2 = 168$, so,

$$a = 23.6/8 = 2.95 \quad \text{and} \quad b = .24167$$

Thus, the least squares line is $\hat{y} = 2.95 + .24167x$. Since 1996 corresponds to $x = 11$, so the prediction for y is

$$\hat{y} = 2.95 + .24167(11) = 5.608$$

11.25 From Exercise 11.9 we form the following table

	x	y	$\hat{y} = 2x$	$(y - \hat{y})^2$	$(\bar{y} - \hat{y})^2$	$(y - \bar{y})^2$
	1	2	2	0	16	16
	2	5	4	1	4	1
	3	4	6	4	0	4
	4	9	8	1	4	9
	5	10	10	0	16	16
Total	15	30	30	6	40	46

Thus, the decomposition of the sum of squares is calculated as $46 = 6 + 40$, and

$$r^2 = 1 - 6/46 = 40/46 = 0.870$$

11.29 The equation obtained in Exercise 11.28 is

$$\hat{y} = 10^{1.452 + .0000666x} = (10^{1.452})(10^{.0000666x}) = 28.314e^{.0001534x}$$

When $x = 3000$, $\hat{y} = 44.86$.

11.33 $y = 3 - 3e^{-\alpha x}$ can be rewritten as

$$\ln(1 - y/3) = -\alpha x$$

Let $y_i' = \ln(1 - y_i/3)$ and $x_i' = -x_i$. Thus, using the no-intercept least square fit

$$\alpha = \frac{\sum x'y'}{\sum x'^2} = \frac{264.3584}{1100} = .240$$

11.37 We wish to minimize

$$D \equiv D(\beta_0, \beta_1, \beta_2) = \sum_{i=1}^{n} [y_i - (\beta_0 + \beta_1 x_{1i} + \beta_2 x_{2i})]^2$$

Taking derivatives

$$\begin{aligned}
\frac{\partial D}{\partial \beta_0} &= -2 \sum_{i=1}^{n} [y_i - (\beta_0 + \beta_1 x_{1i} + \beta_2 x_{2i})] \\
\frac{\partial D}{\partial \beta_1} &= -2 \sum_{i=1}^{n} [y_i - (\beta_0 + \beta_1 x_{1i} + \beta_2 x_{2i})]\, x_{1i} \\
\frac{\partial D}{\partial \beta_2} &= -2 \sum_{i=1}^{n} [y_i - (\beta_0 + \beta_1 x_{1i} + \beta_2 x_{2i})]\, x_{2i}
\end{aligned}$$

Setting these to zero gives

$$\begin{aligned}
\sum y &= nb_0 + b_1 \sum x_1 + b_2 \sum x_2 \\
\sum x_1 y &= b_0 \sum x_1 + b_1 \sum x_1^2 + b_2 \sum x_1 x_2 \\
\sum x_2 y &= b_0 \sum x_2 + b_1 \sum x_1 x_2 + b_3 \sum x_2^2
\end{aligned}$$

11.41 The system of linear equations to be solved is

$$84.6 = 10b_0 + 15.3b_1 + 939b_2$$

$$132.27 = 15.3b_0 + 29.85b_1 + 1{,}458.9b_2$$

$$8{,}320.2 = 939b_0 + 1{,}458.9b_1 + 94{,}131b_2$$

Solving gives the fitted line

$$\hat{y} = 2.266 + 0.225x_1 + 0.0623x_2$$

When $x_1 = 2.2$ and $x_2 = 90$, the predicted value is 8.368.

11.45 (a)

```
READ 'ex.d' C1-C3
 16 ROWS READ
 ROW     C1    C2     C3

   1     41     1      5
   2     49     2      5
   3     69     3      5
   4     65     4      5
   .  .  .

REGRESS C1 ON 2 PREDICTORS IN C2 C3 STORE C4 FIT IN C5;
RESIDUALS C6.

The regression equation is
C1 = 46.4 + 7.78 C2 - 1.65 C3

Predictor       Coef          Stdev       t-ratio
Constant      46.438          3.517         13.20
C2            7.7750         0.9485          8.20
C3           -1.6550         0.1897         -8.72

s = 4.242        R-sq = 91.7%      R-sq(adj) = 90.4%
\newpage
Analysis of Variance

SOURCE        DF          SS            MS
Regression     2      2578.5        1289.3
Error         13       233.9          18.0
Total         15      2812.4
```

SOURCE	DF	SEQ SS
C2	1	1209.0
C3	1	1369.5

```
PLOT C6 VS C5

   8.0+
      -                                        *
C6    -
      -
      -                           *     *
   4.0+                                 *
      -
      -             *      *
      -             *
      -
   0.0+
      -                    *     *
      -                          *
      -       *
      -
  -4.0+                    *                   *      *
      -                           *      *
      -
      -
        --------+---------+---------+---------+---------+-C5
               24        36        48        60        72
```

```
NSCORE C6 SET C7
PLOT C6 VS C7
```

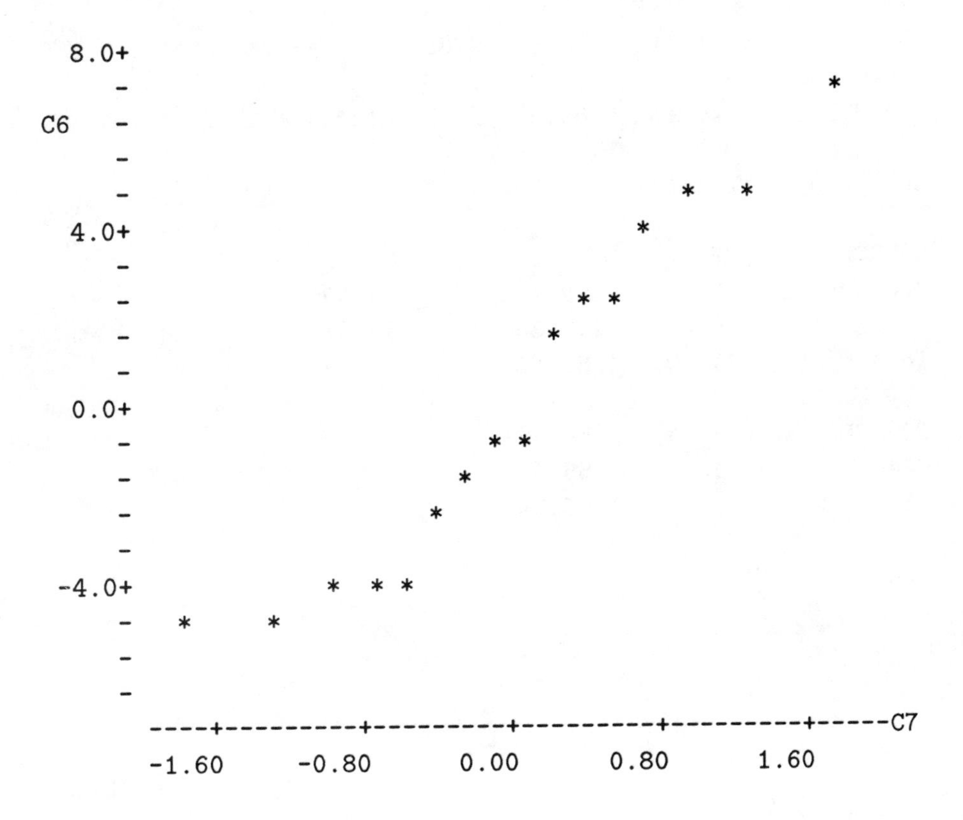


```
(b) READ '11.38.d' C1-C3
    12 ROWS READ
 ROW      C1      C2      C3

   1    78.9    0.02    1000
   2    65.1    0.02    1100
   3    55.2    0.02    1200
   4    56.4    0.02    1300
  .  .  .

REGRESS C1 ON 2 PREDICTORS IN C2 C3 STORE C4 FIT IN C5;
RESIDUALS C6.

The regression equation is
C1 = 161 + 33.0 C2 - 0.0855 C3
```

```
Predictor        Coef          Stdev     t-ratio
Constant       161.34          11.43       14.11
C2              32.97          16.75        1.97
C3          -0.085500       0.009788       -8.74

s = 3.791        R-sq = 89.9%     R-sq(adj) = 87.7%

Analysis of Variance

SOURCE        DF          SS          MS
Regression     2     1152.19      576.09
Error          9      129.34       14.37
Total         11     1281.53

SOURCE        DF      SEQ SS
C2             1       55.65
C3             1     1096.54

PLOT C6 VS C5

     6.0+
        -    *
C6      -
        -
        -                                                    *
     3.0+          *
        -                                            *
        -       *                                        *
        -
        -
     0.0+
        -                                 *
        -                                     *
        -
        -
    -3.0+                            *
        -
        -               *       *
        -                   *
          +---------+---------+---------+---------+---------C5
        49.0      56.0      63.0      70.0      77.0
```

```
NSCORE C6 SET C7
PLOT C6 VS C7
```

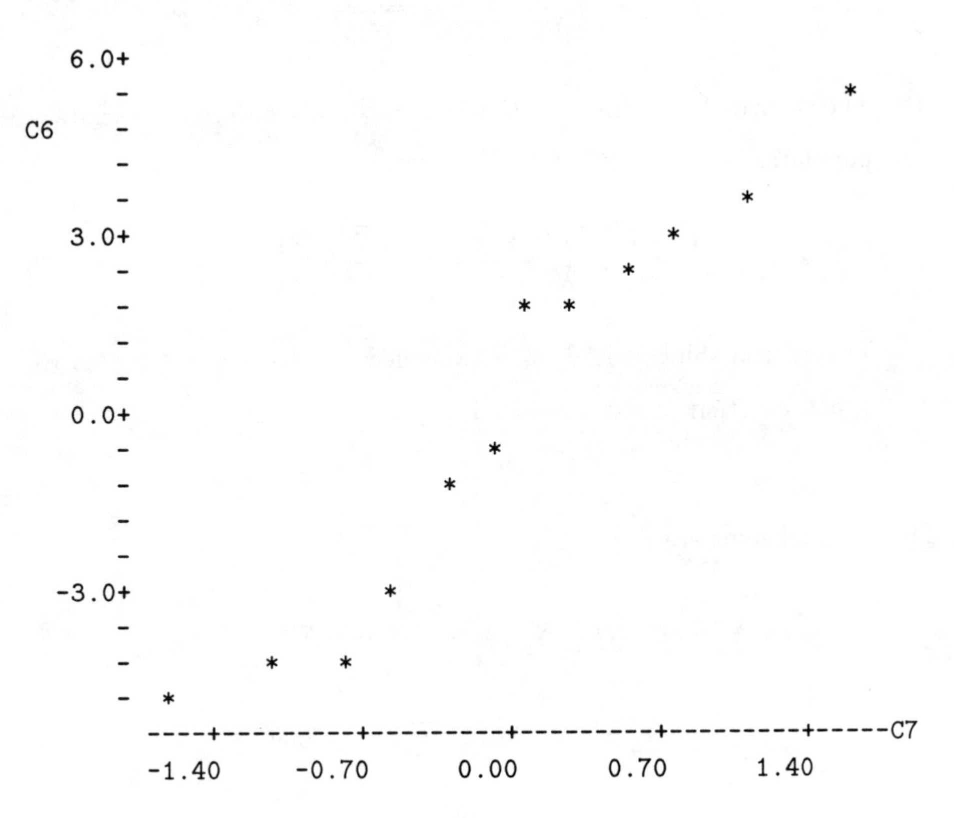

11.49 (a) We first calculate

$$\sum x_i^2 = 532,000, \quad \sum x_i = 2,000, \quad \sum y_i^2 = 9.1097$$

$$\sum y_i = 8.35, \quad \sum x_i y_i = 2175.4$$

So,

$$\begin{aligned} S_{xx} &= 532000 - (2000)^2/10 = 132,000 \\ S_{yy} &= 9.1097 - (8.35)^2/10 = 2.13745 \\ S_{xy} &= 2175.4 - (8.35)(2000)/10 = 505.4 \end{aligned}$$

Thus,

$$r = \frac{505.4}{\sqrt{(132000)(2.13745)}} = 0.9515.$$

(b) The statistic for testing $\rho = 0$, when the data are from a bivariate normal population is

$$Z = \frac{\sqrt{n-3}}{2} \ln\left(\frac{1+r}{1-r}\right) = \frac{\sqrt{7}}{2} \ln\left(\frac{1+.9515}{1-.9515}\right) = 4.89$$

The critical value is 1.96 for a two-sided test with $\alpha = 0.05$, so the null hypothesis that $\rho = 0$ is rejected.

11.53 The required sums are

$$\sum x = 533\ , \ \sum x^2 = 24529\ , \ \sum y = 132$$

$$\sum y^2 = 1526\ , \ \sum xy = 6093$$

$$S_{xx} = 24529 - (533)^2/12 = 854.9167$$

$$S_{yy} = 1526 - (132)^2/12 = 74$$

$$S_{xy} = 6093 - (132)(533)/12 = 230$$

Thus,

$$r = \frac{230}{\sqrt{(854.9167)(74)}} = 0.914$$

$$\mathcal{Z} = \frac{1}{2}\ln\left(\frac{1+r}{1-r}\right) = \frac{1}{2}\ln\left(\frac{1+.914}{1-.914}\right) = 1.554$$

Since $z_{0.025} = 1.96$, the formula

$$\mathcal{Z} - \frac{z_{0.025}}{\sqrt{n-3}} < \mu_{\mathcal{Z}} < \mathcal{Z} + \frac{z_{0.025}}{\sqrt{n-3}}$$

gives a 95 percent interval from 0.9007 to 2.207 for $\mu_{\mathcal{Z}}$. This corresponds to an interval for ρ from 0.7166 to 0.9761.

11.57 (a) Using the formula in Exercise 11.53, $\mathcal{Z} = 0.9076$. Then, using the formula in 11.53 again with $z_{0.025} = 1.96$, the interval for $\mathcal{Z}$ is from 0.4176 to 1.397. The corresponding interval for ρ is from 0.395 to 0.885.

(b) Proceeding as in part (a), $\mathcal{Z} = 0.3654$. The interval for $\mathcal{Z}$ is from -0.0524 to 0.7833. The corresponding interval for ρ is from -0.052 to 0.655.

(c) $\mathcal{Z} = 0.6475$. Thus, the interval for $\mathcal{Z}$ is from 0.3253 to 0.9697. The corresponding interval for ρ is from 0.314 to 0.749.

11.61 (a) Independence always implies that $\rho = 0$. If X and Y are independent, then

$$f(x,y) = f_1(x)f_2(y), \quad \text{and so} \quad f_2(y|x) = \frac{f(x,y)}{f_1(x)} = f_2(y).$$

Therefore, σ^2, the conditional variance of Y given $X = x$, is equal to the variance σ^2 of the marginal distribution of Y and hence,

$$\rho^2 = 1 - \frac{\sigma^2}{\sigma^2} = 1 - 1 = 0.$$

(b)

$$f(x,y) = \frac{1}{2\pi\sigma_1\sigma_2\sqrt{1-\rho^2}} \times$$

$$\exp\left[-\left(\left(\frac{x-\mu_1}{\sigma_1}\right)^2 - 2\rho\left(\frac{x-\mu_1}{\sigma_1}\right)\left(\frac{y-\mu_2}{\sigma_2}\right) + \left(\frac{y-\mu_2}{\sigma_2}\right)^2\right)/2(1-\rho^2)\right]$$

When $\rho = 0$,

$$f(x,y) = \frac{1}{2\pi\sigma_1\sigma_2}\exp\left[-\frac{1}{2}\left[\left(\frac{x-\mu_1}{\sigma_1}\right)^2 + \left(\frac{y-\mu_2}{\sigma_2}\right)^2\right]\right]$$

$$= \frac{1}{\sqrt{2\pi}\sigma_1} \exp\left[-\frac{1}{2}\left(\frac{x-\mu_1}{\sigma_1}\right)^2\right] \times \frac{1}{\sqrt{2\pi}\sigma_2} \exp\left[-\frac{1}{2}\left(\frac{y-\mu_2}{\sigma_2}\right)^2\right]$$
$$= f_1(x) f_2(y)$$

which implies independence.

11.65 (a) Written as ranks, the data in this example are

x	y	d_i^2	x	y	d_i^2
2	1	1	10	9	1
1	4	9	9	5	16
3	3	0	5	8	9
7	10	9	6	6	0
4	2	4	8	7	1

$$r_S = 1 - \frac{6 \sum d_i^2}{n(n^2 - 1)} = 1 - \frac{6(50)}{10(100 - 1)} = 0.697.$$

This is a little smaller than the 0.73 obtained using the sample correlation.

(b) Written as ranks the data in this example are

x	y	d_i^2	x	y	d_i^2
16	10	36	10.5	15	20.25
3	1	4	13	11.5	2.25
17	21	16	10.5	2	72.25
6	13	49	21.5	19	6.25
6	3	9	1.5	6.5	25
21.5	23	2.25	14	21	49
8.5	8	0.25	15	18	9
4	6.5	6.25	6	4.5	2.25
23.5	17	42.25	19.5	15	20.25
8.5	11.5	9	1.5	4.5	9
19.5	24	20.25	23.5	21	6.25
12	9	9	18	15	9

Thus $\sum d_i^2 = 434$ and

$$r_S = 1 - \frac{6 \sum d_i^2}{n(n^2 - 1)} = 1 - \frac{6(434)}{24(24^2 - 1)} = 0.811.$$

This is essentially the same as the .809 obtained from the sample correlation.

(c) Written as ranks, the data in this example are

x	y	d_i^2	x	y	d_i^2
1	1	0	6	5	1
2	3	1	7	8	1
3	2	1	8	9	1
4	6	4	9	7	4
5	4	1	10	10	0

Thus $\sum d_i^2 = 14$ and

$$r_S = 1 - \frac{6 \sum d_i^2}{n(n^2 - 1)} = 1 - \frac{6(14)}{10(100 - 1)} = 0.915.$$

This is also close to, though less than $r = 0.9629$.

11.69
```
READ '11.50.d' IN C1 C2
        24 ROWS READ
 ROW      C1      C2

   1      43      32
   2      29      20
   3      44      45
   4      33      35
   .    .    .

CORR C1 C2

Correlation of C1 and C2 = 0.809
```

11.73 (a) The prediction for the mean repair time at $x = 4.5$ is

$$\hat{y} = a + b(4.5) = 2 + 16(4.5) = 74$$

and the 95 percent confidence interval is

$$74 \pm 3.182\sqrt{680}\sqrt{\frac{1}{5} + \frac{(4.5-3)^2}{10}}.$$

So the interval is from 19.9 hours to 128.1 hours.

(b) The 95 percent limits of prediction for a single engine that is run $x = 4.5$ thousand hours is

$$74 \pm 3.182\sqrt{680}\sqrt{1 + \frac{1}{5} + \frac{(4.5-3)^2}{10}}.$$

So the interval is from 0 hours to 173.1 hours (the lower limit of -25.1 does not make any sense, so we take 0 as the lower limit).

11.77 The ideal gas law is $pV^{\gamma} = C$. Taking logs of both sides gives

$$\ln p + \gamma \ln V = C.$$

Let $y_i = \ln p_i$ and $x_i = -\ln V_i$. Then, $\bar{x} = -2.815$, $\bar{y} = 4.530$, $S_{xx} = 3.3068$, $S_{xy} = 4.9573$. So,

$$\begin{aligned} \gamma &= \frac{S_{xy}}{S_{xx}} = 1.499 \\ C &= \bar{y} - b\bar{x} = 8.760 \end{aligned}$$

11.81 (a) From Exercise 11.9, $S_{xx} = 10$, $S_{xy} = 20$, $S_{yy} = 46$ and $\hat{y} = 0 + 2x$. Also $s_e^2 = 2.00$. The prediction for the mean CPU time at $x = 3.0$ is $\hat{y} = 0 +$

$2(3.0) = 6$. The 95 percent confidence interval is given by

$$6 \pm 3.182\sqrt{2.00}\sqrt{\frac{1}{5} + \frac{(3-3)^2}{10}}.$$

So the interval is from 3.99 to 8.01 hours.

(b) The 95 percent limits of prediction for a single future day is

$$6 \pm 3.182\sqrt{2.00}\sqrt{1 + \frac{1}{5} + \frac{(3-3)^2}{10}}.$$

So the interval is from 1.07 to 10.93 hours.

11.85 (a) Since the transformation $\mathcal{Z} = (1/2)\ln(1 + r/1 - r) = 1.045$ and $z_{0.025} = 1.96$, the 95% confidence interval for $\mathcal{Z}$ is $\mathcal{Z} \pm 1.96/\sqrt{n-3}$ or from 0.4796 to 1.6112. The corresponding interval for ρ is from 0.446 to 0.923 .

(b) Proceeding as in part (a), $\mathcal{Z} = -0.725$. The interval for $\mathcal{Z}$ is from -1.089 to -0.361. The corresponding interval for ρ is from -0.797 to -0.346.

(c) $\mathcal{Z} = 0.1717$. Thus, the interval for $\mathcal{Z}$ is from -0.1748 to 0.5181. The corresponding interval for ρ is from -0.173 to 0.476.

Chapter 12

ANALYSIS OF VARIANCE

12.1 (a) If the experiment is performed in soft water, the results may only be valid in soft water. Other kinds of water should also be used.

(b) With 15 results for detergent A and only 5 for detergent B, the variability for detergent A is known with much more precision than that for detergent B. Equal sample sizes should be used.

(c) The results may only apply to very hot water and very short wash times, and not to the circumstances of normal use with low temperature and longer washing times.

(d) There may be a time effect for the measurement process determining "whiteness"; for example, the instrument may require recalibration after a few readings. The test results may be biased in this case.

12.5 The null hypothesis is that the mean number of mistakes is the same for the four technicians. The alternative is that the means are not the same. The analysis-of-variance table is

Source of variation	Degrees of freedom	Sum of squares	Mean square	F
Technicians	3	12.95	4.3167	0.68
Error	16	101.60	6.3500	
Total	19	114.55		

Since the critical value at the 0.01 level for an F distribution with 3 and 16 degrees of freedom is 5.29, we cannot reject the null hypothesis.

12.9 The null hypothesis is that the true means of the samples of reactions times are the same. The alternative is that the true means are not the same. The analysis-of-variance table is

Source of variation	Degrees of freedom	Sum of squares	Mean square	F
Arrangements	2	81.429	40.7145	11.310
Error	25	90.000	3.600	
Total	27	171.429		

Since the critical value at the 0.01 level for an F distribution with 2 and 25 degrees of freedom is 5.57, we can reject the null hypothesis. The mean reaction times are not the same for the three arrangements.

12.13 Since $\mu_i = \mu + \alpha_i$ and

$$\frac{1}{k}\sum_{i=1}^{k} \mu_i = \mu$$

$$\sum_{i=1}^{k} \alpha_i = \sum_{i=1}^{k} (\mu_i - \mu) = \sum_{i=1}^{k} \mu_i - \sum_{i=1}^{k} \mu = 0$$

12.17

```
AOVONEWAY C1-C3

ANALYSIS OF VARIANCE
SOURCE   DF       SS       MS       F
```

```
FACTOR    2    81.43   40.71   11.31
ERROR    25    90.00    3.60
TOTAL    27   171.43
```

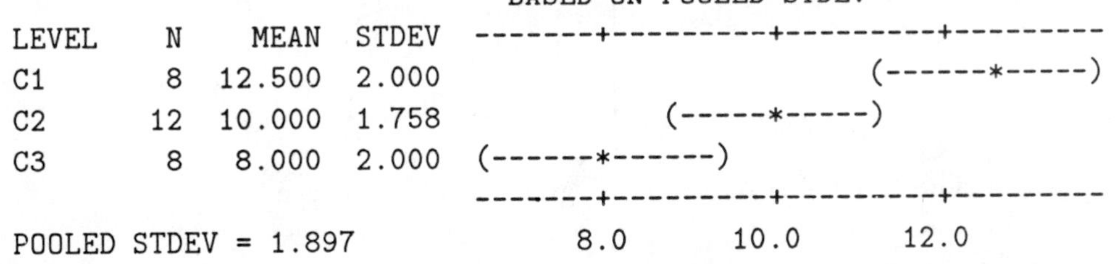

```
                                   INDIVIDUAL 95 PCT CI'S FOR MEAN
                                   BASED ON POOLED STDEV
LEVEL      N     MEAN   STDEV   -------+---------+---------+---------
C1         8   12.500   2.000                             (------*-----)
C2        12   10.000   1.758              (-----*-----)
C3         8    8.000   2.000   (------*------)
                                -------+---------+---------+---------
POOLED STDEV = 1.897                  8.0      10.0      12.0
```

12.21 (a) We first find $a = 4$, $\bar{y}_{..} = 10$, $\bar{y}_{1.} = 8$, $\bar{y}_{2.} = 13$, $\bar{y}_{3.} = 10$ and $\bar{y}_{4.} = 9$. And $b = 5$, $\bar{y}_{.1} = 13$, $\bar{y}_{.2} = 8$, $\bar{y}_{.3} = 12$, $\bar{y}_{.4} = 6$ and $\bar{y}_{.5} = 11$. Thus,

$$\underset{\substack{\text{Obs.}\\ y_{ij}}}{\begin{bmatrix} 14 & 6 & 11 & 0 & 9 \\ 14 & 10 & 16 & 9 & 16 \\ 12 & 7 & 10 & 9 & 12 \\ 12 & 9 & 11 & 6 & 7 \end{bmatrix}} = \underset{\substack{\text{Grand mean}\\ \bar{y}_{..}}}{\begin{bmatrix} 10 & 10 & 10 & 10 & 10 \\ 10 & 10 & 10 & 10 & 10 \\ 10 & 10 & 10 & 10 & 10 \\ 10 & 10 & 10 & 10 & 10 \end{bmatrix}}$$

$$+ \underset{\substack{\text{Tr. effect}\\ \bar{y}_{i.} - \bar{y}_{..}}}{\begin{bmatrix} -2 & -2 & -2 & -2 & -2 \\ 3 & 3 & 3 & 3 & 3 \\ 0 & 0 & 0 & 0 & 0 \\ -1 & -1 & -1 & -1 & -1 \end{bmatrix}} + \underset{\substack{\text{Bl. effect}\\ \bar{y}_{.j} - \bar{y}_{..}}}{\begin{bmatrix} 3 & -2 & 2 & -4 & 1 \\ 3 & -2 & 2 & -4 & 1 \\ 3 & -2 & 2 & -4 & 1 \\ 3 & -2 & 2 & -4 & 1 \end{bmatrix}}$$

Error

$$
+ \overset{y_{ij} - \bar{y}_{i.} - \bar{y}_{.j} + \bar{y}_{..}}{\begin{bmatrix} 3 & 0 & 1 & -4 & 0 \\ -2 & -1 & 1 & 0 & 2 \\ -1 & -1 & -2 & 3 & 1 \\ 0 & 2 & 0 & 1 & -3 \end{bmatrix}}
$$

(b) The sums of squares and degrees of freedoms are

$$
\begin{aligned}
SS(Tr) &= 5(-2)^2 + 5(3)^2 + 5(0)^2 + 5(-1)^2 = 70, \quad df = 3. \\
SS(Bl) &= 4(3)^2 + 4(-2)^2 + 4(2)^2 + 4(-4)^2 + 4(1) = 136, \quad df = 4. \\
SSE &= 3^2 + 0^2 + 1^2 + \cdots + 0^2 + 1^2 + (-3)^2 = 66, \\
& \qquad df = (4-1)(5-1) = 12. \\
SST &= 14^2 + 6^2 + 11^2 + \cdots + 11^2 + 6^2 + 7^2 - 20(10)^2 = 272, \\
& \qquad df = 19 \\
&= SS(Tr) + SS(Bl) + SSE = 272. \quad (check)
\end{aligned}
$$

(c) The null hypothesis is that the four treatment population means are the same. The alternative is that they are not the same. The analysis-of-variance table is

Source of variation	Degrees of freedom	Sum of squares	Mean square	F
Treatments	3	70	23.33	4.24
Blocks	4	136	34.00	6.18
Error	12	66	5.50	
Total	19	272		

Since the critical value at the 0.05 level for an F distribution with 3 and 12 degrees of freedom is 3.49, we can reject the null hypothesis. The treatment means are not the same. Since $F_{.05}$ with 4 and 12 degrees of freedom is 3.26, the block effect of the experiment is also apparent.

12.25 To use the sums of squares formula, we need to compute the marginal and total sums

$$T_{..1} = 438, \quad T_{..2} = 483$$

$$T_{.1.} = 223, \quad T_{.2.} = 236, \quad T_{.3.} = 242, \quad T_{.4.} = 220$$

$$T_{1..} = 308, \quad T_{2..} = 304, \quad T_{3..} = 309, \quad T_{...} = 921$$

Thus, $C = (921)^2/(3 \cdot 4 \cdot 2) = 35,343.375$. Further,

$$\sum_{i=1}^{a} T_{i..}^2 = 308^2 + 304^2 + 309^2 = 282,761$$

$$\sum_{j=1}^{b} T_{.j.}^2 = 223^2 + 236^2 + 242^2 + 220^2 = 212,389$$

$$\sum_{k=1}^{r} T_{..k}^2 = 438^2 + 483^2 = 425,133$$

$$\sum_{i=1}^{a} \sum_{j=1}^{b} \sum_{k=1}^{r} y_{ijk}^2 = 35,715$$

Thus,

$$SST = 35,715 - 35,343.375 = 371.625$$

$$SS(Tr) = \frac{282,761}{4 \cdot 2} - 35,343.375 = 1.750$$

$$SS(Bl) = \frac{212,389}{3 \cdot 2} - 35,343.375 = 54.792$$

$$SS(Reps) = \frac{425,133}{4 \cdot 3} - 35,343.375 = 84.375$$

$$SSE = 371.62 - 1.745 - 54.79 - 84.37 = 230.715$$

The analysis of variance is

Source of variation	Degrees of freedom	Sum of squares	Mean square	F
Machines	2	1.750	0.875	0.064
Workers	3	54.792	18.264	1.364
Reps	1	84.375	84.375	6.217
Error	17	230.708	13.571	
Total	23	371.625		

Since the critical value at the 0.05 level for an F distribution with 2 and 17 degrees of freedom is 3.59, we cannot reject the null hypothesis of no treatment (machine) effect.

Since the critical value at the 0.05 level for an F distribution with 3 and 17 degrees of freedom is 3.20, we cannot reject the null hypothesis of no block(worker) effect.

Since the critical value at the 0.05 level for an F distribution with 1 and 17 degrees of freedom is 3.45 , we reject the null hypothesis of no replication effect.

12.29 From Exercise 12.21, the (sorted) means for the four treatments are

Treatment 1	Treatment 4	Treatment 3	Treatment 2
8	9	10	13

and the $MSE = 5.5$ with 5 degrees of freedom. From Table 12(a), after multiplying each r_p by $s_{\bar{y}} = \sqrt{MSE/n} = \sqrt{5.5/5} = 1.049$ to get R_p, we obtain

p	2	3	4
r_p	3.08	3.23	3.31
R_p	3.23	3.39	3.47

For $\alpha = .05$, none of the ranges between two adjacent means are significant. Only $\bar{y}_2 - \bar{y}_4 = 4$ is significant among the ranges of three adjacent means.

The range of four means $\bar{y}_2 - \bar{y}_1 = 5$ is significant among the ranges of three adjacent means. The range of four means $\bar{y}_2 - \bar{y}_1 = 5 > R_4$ is also significant. We conclude

Tr 1	Tr 4	Tr 3	Tr 2
8	9	10	13

12.33 (a) The (sorted) sample means for the five threads are

thread 1	thread 5	thread 3	thread 4	thread 2
20.675	20.900	23.525	23.700	25.650

and, from Exercise 12.18, the $MSE = 2.110$ with 12 degrees of freedom. From Table 12(b) with 12 degrees of freedom , after multiplying each r_p by $s_{\bar{y}} = \sqrt{MSE/n} = \sqrt{2.110/4} = 0.726$ to get R_p, we obtain

p	2	3	4	5
r_p	4.32	4.50	4.62	4.71
R_p	3.14	3.27	3.35	3.42

We conclude that, at the .01 level of significance, the means of detergents B and C are significantly different but that the means of detergents A and B are not different.

thread 1	thread 5	thread 3	thread 4	thread 2
20.675	20.900	23.525	23.700	25.650

(b) With $k = 5$, $\alpha = .10$ and $\alpha/k(k-1) = .10/20 = .005$, we have $t_{.005} = 3.055$ with 12 degrees of freedom. Using Bonferroni's procedure, we can construct 10 confidence intervals for the differences of mean breaking strength of the five threads and are 90% confidence that all 10 intervals hold simutaneous. For example, the confidence interval for $\mu_1 - \mu_2$ is

$$\mu_1 - \mu_2 \ : \qquad (\bar{y}_{1.} - \bar{y}_{2.}) \pm t_{.005}\sqrt{MSE(\frac{1}{4} + \frac{1}{4})}$$

$$= (20.675 - 25.650) \pm 3.055\sqrt{2.11(\frac{1}{4} + \frac{1}{4})}$$
$$= -4.975 \pm 3.138$$

Similarly, with the same 3.138 applying for all pairs of mean differences, we obtain

$$\begin{aligned}
\mu_1 - \mu_3 &: & (20.675 - 23.525) \pm 3.138 &= -2.850 \pm 3.138 \\
\mu_1 - \mu_4 &: & (20.675 - 23.700) \pm 3.138 &= -3.025 \pm 3.138 \\
\mu_1 - \mu_5 &: & (20.675 - 20.900) \pm 3.138 &= -0.225 \pm 3.138 \\
\mu_2 - \mu_3 &: & (25.650 - 23.525) \pm 3.138 &= 2.125 \pm 3.138 \\
\mu_2 - \mu_4 &: & (25.650 - 23.700) \pm 3.138 &= 1.950 \pm 3.138 \\
\mu_2 - \mu_5 &: & (25.650 - 20.900) \pm 3.138 &= 4.750 \pm 3.138 \\
\mu_3 - \mu_4 &: & (23.525 - 23.700) \pm 3.138 &= -0.175 \pm 3.138 \\
\mu_3 - \mu_5 &: & (23.525 - 20.900) \pm 3.138 &= 2.625 \pm 3.138 \\
\mu_4 - \mu_5 &: & (23.700 - 20.900) \pm 3.138 &= 2.800 \pm 3.138
\end{aligned}$$

Note that only two confidence intervals do not include zero. We are 90% confident that in average, thread 2 is stronger than threads 1 and 5, but also are unable to differentiate between the mean strength of threads 1, 3, 4, and 5 or threads 2, 3 and 4.

12.37 There are four null hypotheses and we test each at the .01 level of significance.

To construct the analysis of variance table, we evaluate the sums of squares.
$C = T_{..}^2/n^2 = 7.78^2/5^2 = 2.421136$

$$SST = \sum_{i=1}^{n}\sum_{j=1}^{n} y_{ij}^2 - C = 2.7648 - 2.421136 = .343664$$

$$SSR = \frac{1}{n}\sum_{k=1}^{n} T_{i.}^2 - C = 2.4852 - 2.421136 = .064064$$

$$SSC = \frac{1}{n}\sum_{j=1}^{n} T_{.j}^2 - C = 2.68772 - 2.421136 = .266584$$

$$SS(Latin) = \frac{1}{n}\sum_{k=1}^{n} T_{(k)}^2 - C = 2.4216 - 2.421136 = .000464$$

$$SS(Greek) = \frac{1}{n}\sum_{l=1}^{n} T_{(l)}^2 - C = 2.4324 - 2.421136 = .011264$$

$$SSE = SST - SS(Latin) - SS(Greek) - SSR - SSC = .001288$$

The analysis-of-variance table is

Source of variation	Degrees of freedom	Sum of squares	Mean square	F
Restraints(Latin)	4	0.000464	0.000116	0.72
Size(Rows)	4	0.064064	0.016016	99.48
Speed(Cols)	4	0.266584	0.066646	413.95
Angle(Greek)	4	0.011264	0.002816	17.49
Error	8	0.001288	0.000161	
Total	24	0.343664		

Since $F_{4,8} = 7.01$ for $\alpha = .01$, we cannot reject the null hypothesis of no mean difference due to restraint system. However, auto size, impact speed and impact angle are all significant.

12.41 The null hypothesis is that track designs are equally resistant to breakage. The level is $\alpha = .01$. The analysis-of-covariance table is

Source of variation	Sum of squares for x	Sum of squares for y	Sum of products
Treatments	420.130	114.55	192.33
Error	556.052	122.40	237.74
Total	976.182	236.95	430.07

Source of variation	Sum of squares for y'	Degrees of freedom	Mean square
Treatments	26.723	3	8.908
Error	20.754	15	1.384
Total	47.477	18	

Thus, the F statistic is 6.44. Since the critical value at the 0.01 level for an F distribution with 3 and 15 degrees of freedom is 5.42, we reject the null hypothesis.

The effect of usage on breakage resistance, that is, the regression coefficient of the model, is given by $SPE/SSE_x = .428$.

12.45 (a) We first find $a = 3$, $\bar{y}_{..} = 9$, $\bar{y}_{1.} = 7$, $\bar{y}_{2.} = 8$ and $\bar{y}_{3.} = 12$. And $b = 4$, $\bar{y}_{.1} = 8$, $\bar{y}_{.2} = 13$, $\bar{y}_{.3} = 4$ and $\bar{y}_{.4} = 11$. Thus,

$$\underset{y_{ij}}{\text{Obs.}} \qquad\qquad \underset{\bar{y}_{..}}{\text{Grand mean}}$$

$$\begin{bmatrix} 9 & 10 & 2 & 7 \\ 6 & 3 & 1 & 12 \\ 9 & 16 & 9 & 14 \end{bmatrix} = \begin{bmatrix} 9 & 9 & 9 & 9 \\ 9 & 9 & 9 & 9 \\ 9 & 9 & 9 & 9 \end{bmatrix}$$

Tr. effect   Bl. effect

$$\bar{y}_{i.} - \bar{y}_{..} \qquad\qquad \bar{y}_{.j} - \bar{y}_{..}$$

$$+\begin{bmatrix} -2 & -2 & -2 & -2 \\ -1 & -1 & -1 & -1 \\ 3 & 3 & 3 & 3 \end{bmatrix} + \begin{bmatrix} -1 & 4 & -5 & 2 \\ -1 & 4 & -5 & 2 \\ -1 & 4 & -5 & 2 \end{bmatrix}$$

Error

$$y_{ij} - \bar{y}_{i.} - \bar{y}_{.j} + \bar{y}_{..}$$

$$+\begin{bmatrix} 3 & -1 & 0 & -2 \\ -1 & 1 & -2 & 2 \\ -2 & 0 & 2 & 0 \end{bmatrix}$$

(b) The sums of squares and degrees of freedoms are

$$\begin{aligned} SS(Tr) &= 4(-2)^2 + 4(-1)^2 + 4(3)^2 = 56, \quad df = 2 \\ SS(Bl) &= 3(-1)^2 + 3(4)^2 + 3(-5)^2 + 3(2)^2 = 138, \quad df = 3 \\ SSE &= 3^2 + (-1)^2 + 0^2 + \cdots + 0^2 + 2^2 + 0^2 = 32, \\ & \qquad df = (3-1)(4-1) = 6 \\ SST &= 9^2 + 10^2 + 2^2 + \cdots + 16^2 + 9^2 + 14^2 - 12(9)^2 = 226, \\ & \qquad df = 11 \\ &= SS(Tr) + SS(Bl) + SSE = 226. \quad (check) \end{aligned}$$

(c) The null hypothesis is that the four treatment population means are the same. The alternative is that they are not the same. A second null hypothesis is that there is no block effect. The analysis-of-variance table is

Source of variation	Degrees of freedom	Sum of squares	Mean square	F
Treatments	2	56	28.00	5.25
Blocks	3	138	46.00	8.63
Error	6	32	5.33	
Total	11	226		

Since the critical value at the 0.05 level for an F distribution with 2 and 6 degrees of freedom is 5.14, we can reject the null hypothesis. The treatment means are not the same. Since $F_{.05}$ with 3 and 6 degrees of freedom is 4.76, the block effect of the experiment is also apparent.

12.49 The null hypotheses are (i) that there is no flow effect and (ii) that there is no precipitator effect. Each will be tested with $\alpha = .01$. Referring to Exercise 12.43, the two-way analysis-of-variance table is

Source of variation	Degrees of freedom	Sum of squares	Mean square	F
Flow	3	0.528	0.1760	7.75
Precipitators	4	0.732	0.1830	8.06
Error	12	0.272	0.0227	
Total	19	1.532		

Since the critical value at the 0.01 level for an F distribution with 3 and 12 degrees of freedom is 5.95, we reject the null hypothesis that there is no flow effect. Since the critical value at the 0.01 level for an F distribution with 4 and 12 degrees of freedom is 5.41, we also reject the null hypothesis that there is no precipitator effect.

The mean square error has dropped to 0.0227 from 0.0628 in the one-way analysis. This drop is to be expected since that variation due to precipitators is no longer pooled into the mean square error.

12.53 The analysis-of-variance table is

Source of variation	Degrees of freedom	Sum of squares	Mean square	F
Designs(Tr)	2	32853.41	16426.71	66.62
Pros(Rows)	2	12007.19	6003.60	24.35
Drivers(Cols)	2	1344.52	672.26	2.73
Fairways(Reps)	2	36140.52	18070.26	73.29
Error	18	4437.99	246.56	
Total	26	86783.63		

Since $F_{2,18} = 6.01$ for $\alpha = .01$, we reject the null hypothesis of no mean difference due to difference in design. We also reject the null hypothesis of no difference among pros and the null hypothesis of no difference among fairways. However, we cannot reject the null hypothesis of no difference among drivers.

We could use the Duncan multiple range test. The (sorted) average distances for the three golf ball designs are

Design C	Design B	Design A
210.56	253.33	296.00

From Table 12(a) with 18 degrees of freedom, after multiplying each r_p by $s_{\bar{y}} = \sqrt{MSE/n} = \sqrt{246.56/9} = 5.234$ to get R_p, we obtain

p	2	3
r_p	2.97	3.12
R_p	15.55	16.33

We conclude that, at the .05 level of significance, the average distance for design A is significantly higher than that of design C and B. designs. And the average distance for design C is significantly lower than design B and A.

Design C	Design B	Design A
210.56	253.33	296.00

Chapter 13

FACTORIAL EXPERIMENTATION

13.1 1. We test each of the following hypotheses.

Null hypothesis (a): The replication effect is zero. $\rho_1 = \rho_2 = \rho_3 = 0$.

We reject the null hypothesis at .05 level if $F > F_{.05} = 4.84$ with 1 and 11 degrees of freedom.

Null hypothesis (b): The two-factor interaction is zero.

We reject the null hypothesis at .05 level if $F > F_{.05} = 2.93$ with 4 and 18 degrees of freedom.

Null hypothesis (c): The temperature(factor B) has no effect. $\beta_1 = \beta_2 = \beta_3 = \beta_4 = \beta_5 = 0$.

We reject the null hypothesis at .05 level if $F > F_{.05} = 2.93$ with 4 and 18 degrees of freedom.

Null hypothesis (d): The concentration(factor A) has no effect. $\alpha_1 = \alpha_2 = 0$.

We reject the null hypothesis at .05 level if $F > F_{.05} = 4.41$ with 1 and 18 degrees of freedom.

2. **Calculations:** The data are

Concentration grams/liter	Temperature (degrees F)	Reflectivity Rep 1	Rep 2	Rep 3	Sum
5	75	35	39	36	110
5	100	31	37	36	104
5	125	30	31	33	94
5	150	28	20	23	71
5	175	19	18	22	59
10	75	38	46	41	125
10	100	36	44	39	119
10	125	39	32	38	109
10	150	35	47	40	122
10	175	30	38	31	99
	Total	321	352	339	1,012

And the table of totals for the two factors are

		Factor B: Temperature(F^0)					
		75	100	125	150	175	
Factor A:	5	110	104	94	71	59	438
Concentration	10	125	119	109	122	99	574
		235	223	203	193	158	1,012

Hence

$$C = \frac{1,012^2}{30} = 34,138.1333$$

And the sum of squares are

$$\begin{aligned}
SST &= \sum_i \sum_j \sum_k y_{ijk}^2 - C = 35,822 - C = 1,683.8667 \\
SS(Tr) &= \frac{1}{r} \sum_i \sum_j T_{ij.}^2 - C = \frac{1}{3}(110^2 + 104^2 + \cdots + 122^2 + 99^2) - C \\
&= 1,403.8667 \\
SSR &= \frac{1}{ab} \sum_k T_{..k}^2 - C = \frac{1}{(2)(5)}(312^2 + 352^2 + 339^2) - C = 48.4667 \\
SSE &= SST - SS(Tr) - SSR = 231.5333
\end{aligned}$$

$$
\begin{aligned}
SSA &= \frac{1}{br}\sum_{i=1}^{a} T_{i..}^2 - C = \frac{1}{(5)(3)}(438^2 + 574^2) - C = 616.5334 \\
SSB &= \frac{1}{ar}\sum_{j=1}^{b} T_{.j.}^2 - C \\
&= \frac{1}{(2)(3)}(235^2 + 223^2 + 203^2 + 193^2 + 158^2) - C = 591.2000 \\
SS(AB) &= SS(Tr) - SSA - SSB = 196.1333
\end{aligned}
$$

The analysis-of-variance table is

Source of variation	Degrees of freedom	Sums of squares	Mean square	F
Replication	2	48.4667	24.2334	1.88
A Concentration	1	616.5334	616.5334	47.93
B Temperature	4	591.2000	147.8000	11.49
AB interaction:	4	196.1333	49.0333	3.81
Error	18	231.5333	12.8630	
Total	29	1683.8667		

3. **Decision:** The replication effect is not significant at .05 level. The concentration effect and the temperature effect are both significant at .05 level. However, these cannot be interpreted individually because the interaction effect is significant at .05 level.

   The two-way table of fitted values, $\bar{y}_{ij.}$, provides a summary of the experiment.

		Factor B: Temperature(F^0)				
		75	100	125	150	175
Factor A:	5	36.67	34.67	31.33	23.67	19.67
Concentration	10	41.67	39.67	36.33	40.67	33.00

4. **Further Analysis:** The optimal reflectivity occurred at 75^0F with concentration 10 grams per liter. At optimal conditions, the reflectivity is a normal random variable with mean μ_{21} and variance σ^2. Since the mean square error(MSE) is an unbiased estimate for σ^2 and $t_{.025} = 2.101$ with 18

degrees of freedom, the 95% confidence interval of reflectivity at optimal conditions is

$$\bar{y}_{21.} \pm t_{.025}\sqrt{\frac{MSE}{n}} = 41.67 \pm 2.101\sqrt{\frac{12.8630}{3}} = 41.67 \pm 4.35$$

or $37.32 < \mu_{21} < 46.02$.

13.5 The table of totals for the two factors are

		Filler			
		32	37	42	
	3	4.09	4.64	5.17	13.90
Flow	12	4.63	4.61	5.13	14.37
	30	4.65	5.11	5.20	14.96
		13.37	14.36	15.50	43.23

We also have $a = 3$, $b = 3$, $r = 2$ and

$$T_{..1} = 21.75, \quad T_{..2} = 21.48, \quad \sum_{i=1}^{3}\sum_{j=1}^{3}\sum_{k=1}^{2} y_{ijk}^2 = 104.4311$$

Hence

$$C = \frac{43.23^2}{(3)(3)(2)} = 103.82405.$$

$$\begin{aligned}
SST &= \sum_i\sum_j\sum_k y_{ijk}^2 - C = 104.43110 - 103.82405 = .60705 \\
SS(Tr) &= \frac{1}{r}\sum_i\sum_j T_{ij.}^2 - C \\
&= \frac{1}{2}(4.09^2 + 4.64^2 + \cdots + 5.11^2 + 5.20^2) - 103.82405 = .55950 \\
SSR &= \frac{1}{ab}\sum_k T_{..k}^2 - C \\
&= \frac{1}{(3)(3)}(21.75^2 + 21.48^2) - 103.82405 = .00405
\end{aligned}$$

$$
\begin{aligned}
SSE &= SST - SS(Tr) - SSR = .04350 \\
SSA &= \frac{1}{br}\sum_{i=1}^{a} T_{i..}^2 - C = \frac{1}{(3)(2)}(13.90^2 + 14.37^2 + 14.96^2) - 103.82405 \\
&= .09403 \\
SSB &= \frac{1}{ar}\sum_{j=1}^{b} T_{.j.}^2 - C = \frac{1}{(3)(2)}(13.37^2 + 14.36^2 + 15.50^2) - 103.82405 \\
&= .37870 \\
SS(AB) &= SS(Tr) - SSA - SSB = .08677
\end{aligned}
$$

The analysis-of-variance table is

Source of variation	Degrees of freedom	Sums of squares	Mean square	F
Replication	1	.00405	.00405	.74
A (Flow)	2	.09403	.04702	8.65
B (Filler)	2	.37870	.18935	34.82
AB interaction:	4	.08677	.02169	3.99
Error	8	.04350	.00544	
Total	17	.60705		

Since $F_{.05} = 5.32$ with 1 and 8 degrees of freedom, the replication effect is not significant at the .05 level. Since $F_{.01} = 8.65$ with 2 and 8 degrees of freedom, the Flow and Filler effects are both significant at .01 level. Since $F_{.05} = 3.84$ with 4 and 8 degrees of freedom, the Flow–Filter interaction effect is also significant at .05 level.

13.9 The four equations are:

$$
\begin{aligned}
\mu_{111} &= \mu + \alpha_1 + \beta_1 + (\alpha\beta)_{11} \\
\mu_{121} &= \mu + \alpha_1 - \beta_1 - (\alpha\beta)_{11} \\
\mu_{211} &= \mu - \alpha_1 + \beta_1 - (\alpha\beta)_{11} \\
\mu_{221} &= \mu - \alpha_1 - \beta_1 + (\alpha\beta)_{11}
\end{aligned}
$$

Now solve the equations by combining the four population means on the left hand sides. We first sum the means.

$$\tfrac{1}{4}(\mu_{111}+\mu_{121}+\mu_{211}+\mu_{221})=\mu$$
$$\tfrac{1}{4}(\mu_{111}+\mu_{121}-\mu_{211}-\mu_{221})=\alpha_1$$
$$\tfrac{1}{4}(\mu_{111}-\mu_{121}+\mu_{211}-\mu_{221})=\beta_1$$
$$\tfrac{1}{4}(\mu_{111}-\mu_{121}-\mu_{211}+\mu_{221})=(\alpha\beta)_{11}$$

13.13 The table of calculations using the Yates' method is given in the first table. The table for analysis-of-variance follows.

Yates' method for Exercise 13.13

Exp. con.	Tr. total	1	2	3	4	Sum of squares
1	82.2	157.7	337.3	690.6	1376.6	59,219.6113
a	75.5	179.6	353.3	686.0	−44.2	61.0513
b	98.4	166.5	352.5	−5.2	92.6	267.9612
ab	81.2	186.8	333.5	−39.0	25.8	20.8013
c	84.3	164.5	−23.9	42.2	−3.0	.2813
ac	82.2	188.0	18.7	50.4	58.2	105.8513
bc	83.0	153.3	−27.3	12.4	1.8	.1013
abc	103.8	180.2	−11.7	13.4	76.6	183.3612
d	82.0	−6.7	21.9	16.0	−4.6	.6613
ad	82.5	−17.2	20.3	−19.0	−33.8	35.7013
bd	107.9	−2.1	23.5	42.6	8.2	2.1013
abd	80.1	20.8	26.9	15.6	1.0	.0313
cd	83.3	.5	−10.5	−1.6	−35.0	38.2813
acd	70.0	−27.8	22.9	3.4	−27.0	22.7813
bcd	89.3	−13.3	−28.3	33.4	5.0	.7813
abcd	90.9	1.6	14.9	43.2	9.8	3.0013

The analysis-of-variance table is

Source of variation	Degrees of freedom	Sums of squares	Mean square	F
Replication	1	300.1250	300.1250	.0046
Main effects:				
A	1	61.0513	61.0513	1.8468
B	1	267.9612	267.9612	8.1057
C	1	.2813	.2813	.0085
D	1	.6613	.6613	.0200
Two-factor interactions:				
AB	1	20.8013	20.8013	.6292
AC	1	105.8513	105.8513	3.2020
AD	1	35.7013	35.7013	1.0799
BC	1	.1013	.1013	.0030
BD	1	2.1013	2.1013	.0636
CD	1	38.2813	38.2813	1.1580
Three-factor interactions:				
ABC	1	183.3612	183.3612	5.5466
ABD	1	.0313	.0313	.0091
ACD	1	22.7813	22.7813	.6891
BCD	1	.7813	.7813	.0236
$ABCD$ interaction:	1	3.0013	3.0013	.0908
Error	15	495.8750	33.0583	
Total	31	1,538.7487		

The critical value is $F_{.05} = 4.54$ with 1 and 15 degrees of freedom. The replication effect is significant at the .05 level and so are the main effect of B and the ABC interaction. It seems that aging time has no effect on the gain of the semiconductor device.

13.17 Multiplying each of the equations in the previous exercise by the appropriate sign and adding gives

$$-(1) + (a) - (b) + (ab) - (c) + (ac) - (bc) + (abc) = -8r\alpha_0 + \epsilon_A$$

where

$$\epsilon_A = \sum_{l=1}^{r} (-\epsilon_{000l} + \epsilon_{100l} - \epsilon_{010l} + \epsilon_{110l} - \epsilon_{001l} + \epsilon_{101l} - \epsilon_{101l} + \epsilon_{111l})$$

and

$$(1) + (a) - (b) - (ab) - (c) - (ac) + (bc) + (abc) = 8r(\beta\gamma)_{00} + \epsilon_{BC}$$

where

$$\epsilon_{BC} = \sum_{l=1}^{r} (\epsilon_{000l} + \epsilon_{100l} - \epsilon_{010l} - \epsilon_{110l} - \epsilon_{001l} - \epsilon_{101l} + \epsilon_{101l} + \epsilon_{111l})$$

13.21 (a) We verify the calculation of mean square using the formulas based on totals.

$$T_{1.} = 24, T_{2.} = 40, T_{3.} = 32, T_{4.} = 44, \text{and } \; T_{..} = 40$$

so $C = 140^2/8 = 2,450$. Further

$$T_{.1} = 68, T_{.2} = 72, \text{and } \; \sum\sum y_{ij}^2 = 2,588$$

so

$$\begin{aligned} SST &= 2,588 - 2,450 = 138 \\ SS(Tr) &= \frac{1}{2}(5,136) - 2,450 = 118 \end{aligned}$$

Therefore $SSE = 138 - 118 = 20$ with 4 degrees of freedom and $MSE = 20/4 = 5$ which verifies the result in the example.

(b)

$$\frac{[B]}{2r} = \frac{1}{2r}[-(1) - (a) + (b) + (ab)]$$

$$= \frac{1}{2r}[-\sum_{k=1}^{r} y_{00k} - \sum_{k=1}^{r} y_{10k} + \sum_{k=1}^{r} y_{01k} + \sum_{k=1}^{r} y_{11k}]$$

$$= \frac{1}{2r}[-\sum_{i=0}^{1}\sum_{k=1}^{r} y_{i0k} + \sum_{i=0}^{1}\sum_{k=1}^{r} y_{i1k}] = \bar{y}_{.1.} - \bar{y}_{.0.}$$

(c)

$$\frac{[AB]}{2r} = \frac{1}{2r}[(1) - (a) - (b) + (ab)]$$

$$= \frac{1}{2r}[\sum_{k=1}^{r} y_{00k} - \sum_{k=1}^{r} y_{10k} - \sum_{k=1}^{r} y_{01k} + \sum_{k=1}^{r} y_{11k}]$$

$$= \frac{1}{2}[\frac{1}{r}\sum_{k=1}^{r} y_{00k} - \frac{1}{r}\sum_{k=1}^{r} y_{10k} - \frac{1}{r}\sum_{k=1}^{r} y_{01k} + \frac{1}{r}\sum_{k=1}^{r} y_{11k}]$$

$$= \frac{1}{2}(\bar{y}_{11.} + \bar{y}_{00.}) - \frac{1}{2}(\bar{y}_{10.} + \bar{y}_{01.})$$

13.25 The visual summary of the eight treatment means is given in Figure 13.1. According to visual procedure, we assume that there is no replication effects in the model. The error sum of squares is

$$SSE = \sum_{i=0}^{1}\sum_{j=0}^{1}\sum_{k=0}^{1}\sum_{l=1}^{r}(y_{ijkl} - \bar{y}_{ijk.})^2$$

with $2^3(r-1)$ degrees of freedom. Thus we calculate

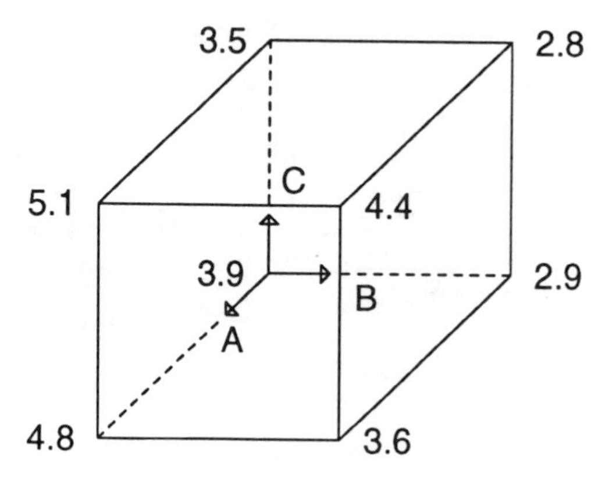

Figure 13.1: Visual summary of the experiment. Exercise 13.25

	Rep. 1	Rep. 2	Mean	$y_{ijk1} - \bar{y}_{ijk.}$	$y_{ijk2} - \bar{y}_{ijk.}$
1	3.7	4.1	3.9	$-.2$	.2
a	4.6	5.0	4.8	$-.2$	.2
b	3.1	2.7	2.9	.2	$-.2$
ab	3.4	3.8	3.6	$-.2$	.2
c	3.4	3.6	3.5	$-.1$	.1
ac	5.3	4.9	5.1	.2	$-.2$
bc	2.4	3.2	2.8	$-.4$	$-.4$
abc	4.7	4.1	4.4	.3	$-.3$
Mean	3.825	3.925	3.875		

Note that $y_{ijk1} - \bar{y}_{ijk.} = -(y_{ijk2} - \bar{y}_{ijk.})$. Squaring the entries in the last two columns and summing, or taking twice the sum of squares for one column, we obtain

$$SSE = 2((-.2)^2 + (-.2)^2 + \cdots + .3^2) = .92$$

with $2^3(2-1) = 8$ degrees of freedom. Therefore, $s^2 = MSE = 92/8 = .115$. Since $t_{.025} = 2.306$ for 8 degrees of freedom, the half length of the confidence intervals is

$$t_{.025}\sqrt{\frac{s^2}{2r}} = 2.306\sqrt{\frac{.115}{4}} = .39$$

The estimated effects are:

Factor A :

$$\bar{y}_{1...} - \bar{y}_{0...} = 4.475 - 3.275 = 1.20$$

Factor B :

$$\bar{y}_{.1..} - \bar{y}_{.0..} = 3.425 - 4.325 = -.90$$

Factor C :

$$\bar{y}_{..1.} - \bar{y}_{..0.} = 3.950 - 3.800 = .150$$

AB :

$$\frac{1}{2}(\bar{y}_{11..} - \bar{y}_{10..} - \bar{y}_{01..} + \bar{y}_{00..}) = \frac{1}{2}(4.0 - 4.95 - 2.85 + 3.7) = -.05$$

AC :

$$\frac{1}{2}(\bar{y}_{1.1.} - \bar{y}_{1.0.} - \bar{y}_{0.1.} + \bar{y}_{0.0.}) = \frac{1}{2}(4.75 - 4.2 - 3.15 + 3.4) = .4$$

BC :

$$\frac{1}{2}(\bar{y}_{.11.} - \bar{y}_{.10.} - \bar{y}_{.01.} + \bar{y}_{.00.}) = \frac{1}{2}(3.6 - 3.25 - 4.3 + 4.35) = .2$$

ABC :

$$\frac{1}{4}(\bar{y}_{111.} - \bar{y}_{101.} - \bar{y}_{011.} + \bar{y}_{001.}) - \frac{1}{4}(\bar{y}_{110.} - \bar{y}_{100.} - \bar{y}_{010.} + \bar{y}_{000.})$$

$$= \frac{1}{4}(4.4 - 5.1 - 2.8 + 3.5) - \frac{1}{4}(3.6 - 4.8 - 2.9 + 3.9) = .05$$

so the confidence intervals are:

(Viscosity) A :

$$1.2 \pm .39 \quad \text{or} \quad .81 \text{ to } 1.59$$

(Temperature) B :

$$-.9 \pm .39 \quad \text{or} \quad -1.29 \text{ to } -.51$$

(Additive) C :

$$.15 \pm .39 \quad \text{or} \quad -.24 \text{ to } .54$$

AB :

$$-.05 \pm .39 \quad \text{or} \quad -.44 \text{ to } .34$$

AC :

$$.4 \pm .39 \quad \text{or} \quad .01 \text{ to } .79$$

BC :

$$.2 \pm .39 \quad \text{or} \quad -.19 \text{ to } .59$$

ABC :

$$.05 \pm .39 \quad \text{or} \quad -.34 \text{ to } .44$$

Only the confidence intervals for the main effects of oil viscosity and temperature and the viscosity $\times$ additive interaction fail to cover 0. Over the conditions of this experiment, low temperature produce a higher mean for the response.

13.29 (a) Since,

$$(a-1)(b-1)(c-1)(d-1)$$

$$= abcd - acd - bcd + cd - abd + ad + bd - d$$

$$-abc + ac + bc - c + ab - a - b + 1$$

we can use the blocks

$$Block\ 1 : 1, ab, ac, bc, bd, ad, cd, abcd$$

$$Block\ 2 : a, b, c, abc, d, abd, bcd, acd$$

(b) Since

$$(a-1)(b-1)(c-1)(d+1)$$

$$= abcd - acd - bcd + cd - abd + ad + bd - d$$

$$+abc - ac - bc + c - ab + a + b - 1$$

we first divide into two blocks

$$Block\ 1 : 1, ab, ac, bc, d, abd, bcd, acd$$

$$Block\ 2 : a, b, c, abc, bd, ad, cd, abcd$$

Since

$$(a+1)(b-1)(c-1)(d-1)$$

$$= abcd - acd + bcd - cd - abd + ad - bd + d$$

$$-abc + ac - bc + c + ab - a + b - 1$$

we divide the two blocks above to get the required 4 blocks.

$$Block\ 1 : 1, bc, abd, acd$$

$$Block\ 2 : ab, ac, d, bcd$$

$$Block\ 3 : a, bd, cd, abc$$

$$Block\ 4 : b, ad, c, abcd$$

13.33 The method of Exercise 13.20 allows the sign of any treatment total to be determined in the sum for any effect total. The odd-even method allows separation of the treatment totals according to sign. Thus, we must show that all "evens" have the same sign and all "odds" have the opposite sign. But the sign for a treatment total in the expansion of the appropriate product is -1 raised to the number of letters in the effect that are not in the treatment total. For example, for effect AB , the sign of (acd) is -1 since there is one letter (B) in AB that is not in (acd). Thus, "evens" must all have the same signs, and "odds" must have the opposite sign.

13.37 (a) The modified standard order is:

$$1, af, bf, ab, cf, ac, bc, abcf, df, ad, bd, abdf, cd, acdf,$$

$$bcdf, aabcd, ef, ae, be, aabef, ce, acef, bcef, abce, de,$$

$$adef, bdef, abde, cdef, acde, bcde, abcdef.$$

(b) The procedure for a 2^n factorial experiment is the same as for the 2^6 case. First write out the 2^{n-1} treatment conditions for the first $n-1$ letters. Then, append the n-th letter to these 2^{n-1} treatment combinations as required to obtain the same treatments as in the half replicate block being used.

13.41 First, we arrange the data in modified standard order and calculate the following table:

Experimental conditions	Rep. 1	Rep 2.	Difference	$(y_1 - y_2)^2/2$
1	39.0	43.2	−4.2	8.82
ad	42.0			
bd	54.9			
ab	40.9	40.3	0.6	0.18
cd	43.1			
ac	29.3			
bc	34.8	48.2	−13.4	89.78
abcd	41.4	49.5	−8.1	32.805

The error sum of squares, obtained by summing the last column of the table, is

$$8.82 + 0.18 + 89.78 + 32.805 = 131.585$$

There are 4 degrees of freedom so the mean squared error is

$$\frac{131.585}{4} = 32.896$$

We use Yates methods to calculate effect totals. Similar to Exercise 13.38, we put the appended letter in parentheses to keep in mind that it has nothing to do with the effect totals calculated.

Yates' method for Exercise 13.41

Exp. con.	Tr. total	1	2	3	Sum of squares
1	39.0	81.0	176.8	325.4	13235.645
$a(d)$	42.0	95.8	148.6	−18.2	41.405
$b(d)$	54.9	72.4	−11.0	18.6	43.245
ab	40.9	76.2	−7.2	3.4	1.445
$c(d)$	43.1	3.0	14.8	−28.2	99.405
ac	29.3	−14.0	3.8	3.8	1.805
bc	34.8	−13.8	−17.0	−11.0	15.125
$abc(d)$	41.4	6.6	20.4	37.4	174.845

The analysis-of-variance table is

Source of variation	Degrees of freedom	Sums of squares	Mean square	F
Main effects:				
$A = BCD$	1	41.405	41.405	1.259
$B = ACD$	1	43.245	43.245	1.315
$C = ABD$	1	99.405	99.405	3.022
$D = ABC$	1	174.845	174.845	5.315
$AB = CD$	1	1.445	1.445	0.044
$AC = BD$	1	1.805	1.805	0.055
$BC = AD$	1	15.125	15.125	0.460
Error	4	131.585	32.896	
Total	11	508.860		

The critical value is $F_{.05} = 7.71$ with 1 and 4 degrees of freedom. None of the effects or interactions is significant at the 5 percent level .

13.45 The table of $\bar{y}_{ij.}$ for the two factors are

		B: 1	2	3	$\bar{y}_{i..}$
A	1	32	16	18	22
	2	14	26	20	20
	$\bar{y}_{.j.}$	23	21	19	

We also have $a = 2$, $b = 3$, $r = 2$ and

$$\bar{y}_{..1} = 19.3333 \ , \quad \bar{y}_{..2} = 22.6667 \ , \quad \bar{y}_{...} = 21$$

Consequently, in each array and summing, we obtain

$$\begin{aligned}
SST &= \sum_{i=1}^{2}\sum_{j=1}^{3}\sum_{k=1}^{2}(y_{ijk} - \bar{y}_{...})^2 \\
&= 8^2 + 14^2 + \cdots + (-5)^2 + 3^2 \ = \ 548 \\
SSA &= (2)(3)\sum_{i=1}^{2}(\bar{y}_{i..} - \bar{y}_{...})^2 \ = \ 6\left(1^2 + (-1)^2\right) \ = \ 12 \\
SSB &= (2)(2)\sum_{j=1}^{3}(\bar{y}_{.j.} - \bar{y}_{...})^2 \ = \ 4\left(2^2 + 0^2 + (-2)^2\right) \ = \ 32
\end{aligned}$$

$$SSR = (2)(3)\sum_{k=1}^{2}(\bar{y}_{..k} - \bar{y}_{...})^2 = 6\left((-1.6667)^2 + 1.6667^2\right) = 33.3347$$

$$SS(AB) = 2\sum_{i=1}^{2}\sum_{j=1}^{3}(\bar{y}_{ij.} - \bar{y}_{i..} - \bar{y}_{.j.} + \bar{y}_{...})^2$$

$$= 2\left(8^2 + (-6)^2 + (-2)^2 + (-8)^2 + 6^2 + 2^2\right) = 416$$

$$SSE = SST - SSA - SSB - SSR - SS(AB) = 54.6653$$

The analysis-of-variance table is

Source of variation	Degrees of freedom	Sums of squares	Mean square	F
Replication	1	33.3347	33.3347	3.05
A	1	12.0000	12.0000	1.10
B	2	32.0000	16.0000	1.46
AB interaction:	2	416.0000	208.0000	19.03
Error	5	54.6653	10.9331	
Total	11	548.0000		

Since $F_{.05} = 6.61$ with 1 and 5 degrees of freedom, and $F_{.05} = 5.79$ with 2 and 5 degrees of freedom, only the AB interaction is significant at .05 level.

13.49 Using the table in Exercise 13.47, we have

$$SST = \sum_{i=0}^{1}\sum_{j=0}^{1}\sum_{l=1}^{r}(y_{ijl} - \bar{y}_{...})^2$$

$$= (-7.75)^2 + (-3.75)^2 + \cdots + 6.75^2 + 7.75^2 = 298.25$$

$$SS(Tr) = r\sum_{i=0}^{1}\sum_{j=0}^{1}(\bar{y}_{ij.} - \bar{y}_{...})^2$$

$$= 3((-6.75)^2 + (-1.75)^2 + (3.25)^2 + (5.25)^2) = 260.25$$

We use the Yates' method to calculate the sum of squares of factors and interactions.

Yates' method for Exercise 13.49				
Exp. con.	Tr. total	1	2	Sum of squares
1	33	96	213	3,780.75
a	63	117	51	216.75
b	48	30	21	36.75
ab	69	21	−9	6.75

The analysis-of-variance table is

Source of variation	Degrees of freedom	Sums of squares	Mean square	F
A	1	216.75	216.75	45.63
B	1	36.75	36.75	7.74
AB	1	6.75	6.75	1.42
Error	8	38.00	4.75	
Total	11	298.25		

The critical values are $F_{.05} = 5.32$ and $F_{.01} = 11.30$, each with 1 and 8 degrees of freedom. The effect for A is significant at the .01 level. The effect for B is significant at the .05 level.

13.53 (a) The four blocks are

Block 1: $a,\ abc,\ bd,\ cd,\ be,\ ce,\ ade,\ abcde$

Block 2: $b,\ c,\ ad,\ abcd,\ ae,\ abce,\ bde,\ cde$

Block 3: $ab,\ ac,\ d,\ bcd,\ e,\ bce,\ abde,\ acde$

Block 4: $1,\ bc,\ abd,\ acd,\ abe,\ ace,\ de,\ bcde$

(b) The block totals are(see Exercise 13.12):

Block 1:	Rep 1:	$4 + 2 + 3 + 10 + 11 + 4 + 15 + 16 = 65$
	Rep 2:	$9 + 4 + 7 + 6 + 5 + 8 + 9 + 11 = 59$
Block 2:	Rep 1:	$2 + 2 + 8 + 11 + 7 + 17 + 4 + 17 = 68$
	Rep 2:	$8 + 5 + 2 + 15 + 4 + 23 + 11 + 11 = 79$
Block 3:	Rep 1:	$15 + 11 + 0 + 6 + 3 + 4 + 10 + 5 = 54$
	Rep 2:	$7 + 6 + 3 + 14 + 7 + 8 + 6 + 10 = 61$
Block 4:	Rep 1:	$3 + 4 + 5 + 6 + 10 + 19 + 7 + 14 = 68$
	Rep 2:	$1 + 1 + 12 + 1 + 17 + 13 + 4 + 9 = 58$

Thus, $C = 512^2/64 = 4{,}096$ and the $SS(Bl) = 33{,}196/8 - 4{,}096 = 53.5$.

The analysis-of-variance table is

Source of variation	Degrees of freedom	Sums of squares 10^{-6}	Mean square 10^{-6}	F
Blocks	7	53.5000	7.6430	.5900
Main Effects:				
A	1	182.2500	182.2500	12.70
B	1	81.0000	81.0000	5.64
C	1	85.5625	85.5625	5.96
D	1	9.0000	9.0000	.63
E	1	248.0625	248.0625	17.28
Unconfounded Interactions:				
AB	1	16.0000	16.0000	1.17
AC	1	3.0625	3.0625	.21
AD	1	90.2500	90.2500	6.29
AE	1	7.5625	7.5625	.53
BC	1	7.5625	7.5625	.53
BD	1	1.0000	1.0000	.07
BE	1	.5625	.5625	.04
CD	1	22.5625	22.5625	1.57
CE	1	30.2500	30.2500	2.11
DE	1	10.5625	10.5625	.74
ABD	1	1.0000	1.0000	.07
ABE	1	3.0625	3.0625	.21
ACD	1	68.0625	68.0625	4.74
ACE	1	25.0000	25.0000	1.74
BCD	1	60.0625	60.0625	4.18
BCE	1	4.0000	4.0000	.28
BDE	1	60.0625	60.0625	4.18
CDE	1	36.0000	36.0000	2.51
$ABCD$	1	52.5625	52.5625	3.66
$ABCE$	1	9.0000	9.0000	.63
$ABDE$	1	18.0625	18.0625	1.26
$ACDE$	1	42.2500	42.2500	2.94
$ABCDE$	1	.2500	.2500	.02
Intrablock Error	28	401.8750	14.3527	
Total	63	1630.0000		

The critical value is $F_{.05} = 4.20$ with 1 and 28 degrees of freedom. The effects for A, B, C, E and AD, ACD interactions are significant at the .05 level. The results is similar to that of Exercise 13.12.

Chapter 14

THE STATISTICAL CONTENT OF QUALITY IMPROVEMENT PROGRAMS

14.1 (a) The center line for the $\bar{x}$ chart is given by $y = \mu = 0.150$. The lower control limit is given by

$$y = 0.150 - \frac{3}{\sqrt{5}}(0.002) = 0.147$$

and the upper control limit is given by

$$y = 0.150 + \frac{3}{\sqrt{5}}(0.002) = 0.153.$$

(b) The center line for the R chart is given by $y = d_2\sigma = 2.326(0.002) = 0.005$. The lower control limit is given by $y = D_1\sigma = 0(0.002) = 0$ and the upper control limit is given by $y = D_2\sigma = 4.918(0.002) = 0.010$.

(c) The control charts are given in the Figures 14.1 and 14.2. For the $\bar{x}$ chart, points at 8, 16, and 17 are outside the limits. For the R chart , all points are within the limits.

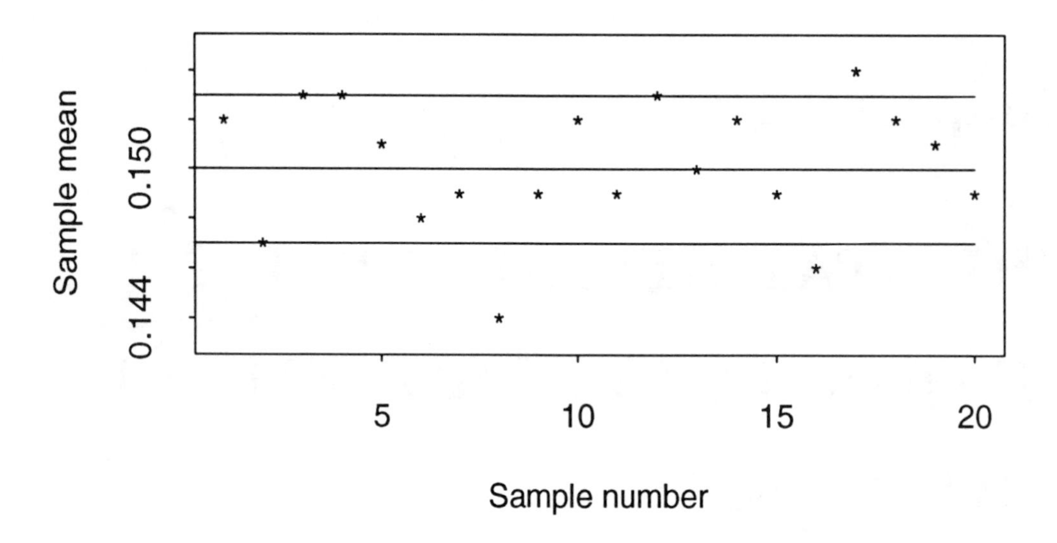

Figure 14.1: Control chart for sample means for Exercise 14.1.

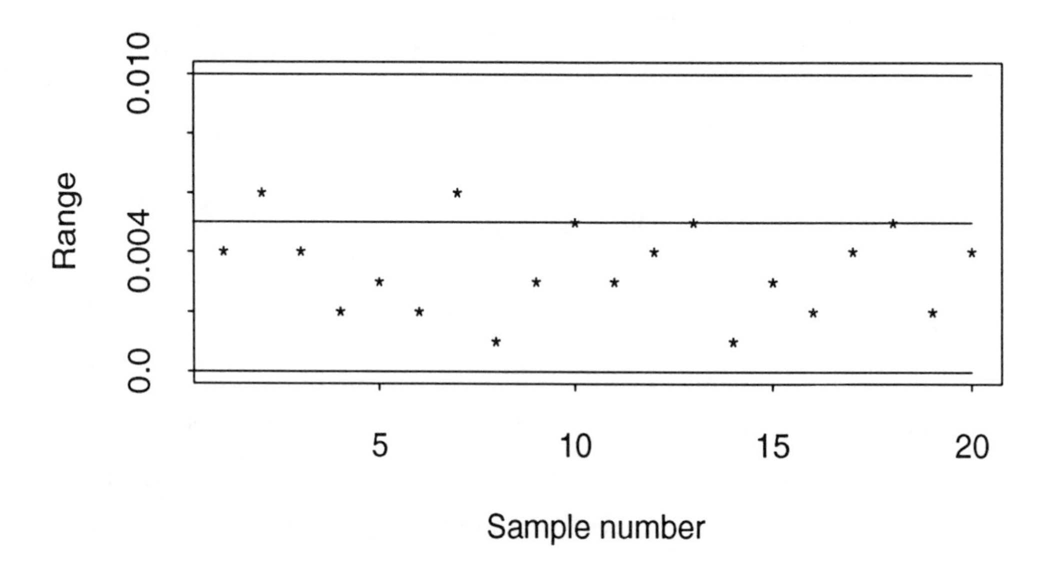

Figure 14.2: Control chart for sample ranges for Exercise 14.1.

14.5 (a) We calculate $\bar{\bar{x}} = 21.7$, $\bar{s} = 1.455$. Thus, for the $\bar{x}$ chart, the center line is 21.7 and

$$LCL = \bar{\bar{x}} - A_1\bar{s} = 21.7 - 2.394(1.455) = 18.22$$

$$UCL = \bar{\bar{x}} + A_1\bar{s} = 21.7 + 2.394(1.455) = 25.18$$

The σ chart has center line $c_2\bar{s} = .72356\ (\ 1.455) = 3.736$

$$LCL = B_3\bar{s} = 0(1.445) = 0$$

$$UCL = B_4\bar{s} = 2.568(1.445) = 3.736$$

The control charts are given in Figures 14.3 and 14.4. All of the sample means are within the control limits. Only one sample standard deviation is outside the control limits, namely the one for the $17th$ sample.

(b) Yes. The process is in control.

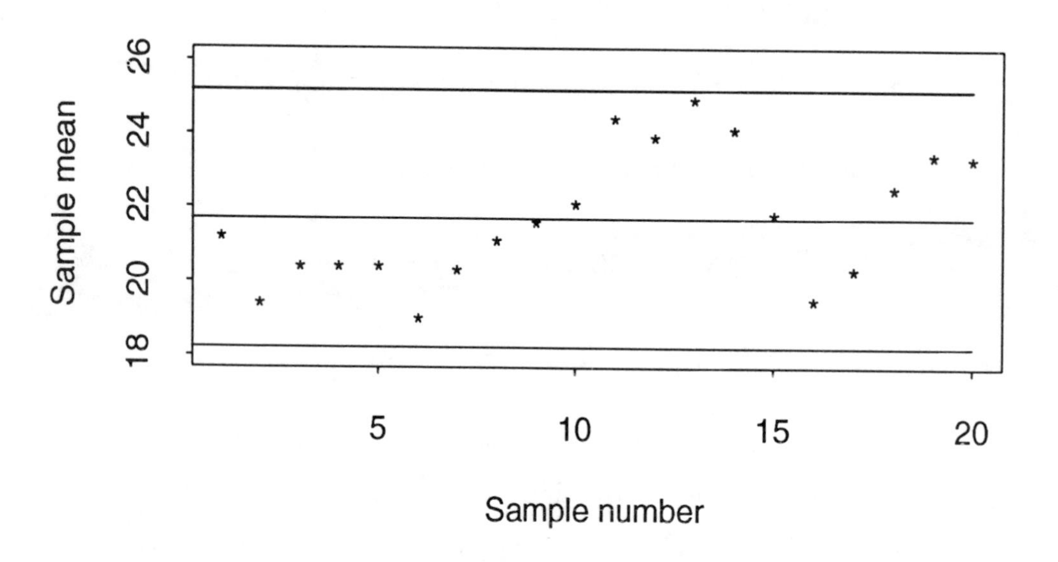

Figure 14.3: Control chart for the sample means for Exercise 14.5.

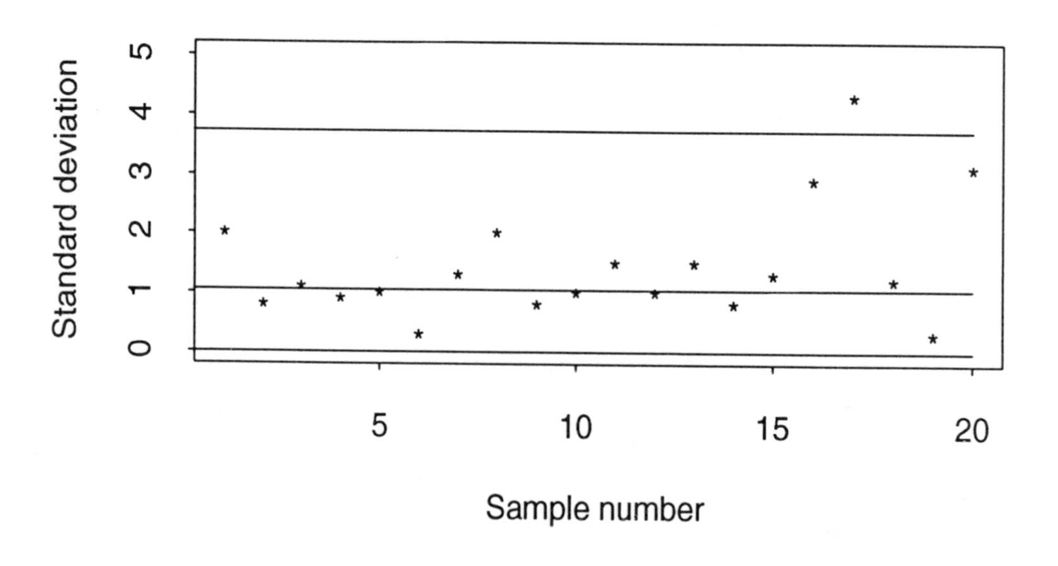

Figure 14.4: Control chart for the sample standard deviations for Exercise 14.5.

14.9 (a) For the data of Exercise 14.8, $\bar{p} = 0.0369$. Thus,

$$\begin{aligned} LCL &= \bar{p} - 3\sqrt{\bar{p}(1-\bar{p})/100} \\ &= 0.0369 - 3\sqrt{0.0369(1-0.0369)/100} = -0.020 \end{aligned}$$

which is taken to be 0, and

$$\begin{aligned} UCL &= \bar{p} + 3\sqrt{\bar{p}(1-\bar{p})/100} \\ &= 0.0369 + 3\sqrt{0.0369(1-0.0369)/100} = 0.0935 \end{aligned}$$

(b) The control chart is given in Figure 14.5. The process is in control.

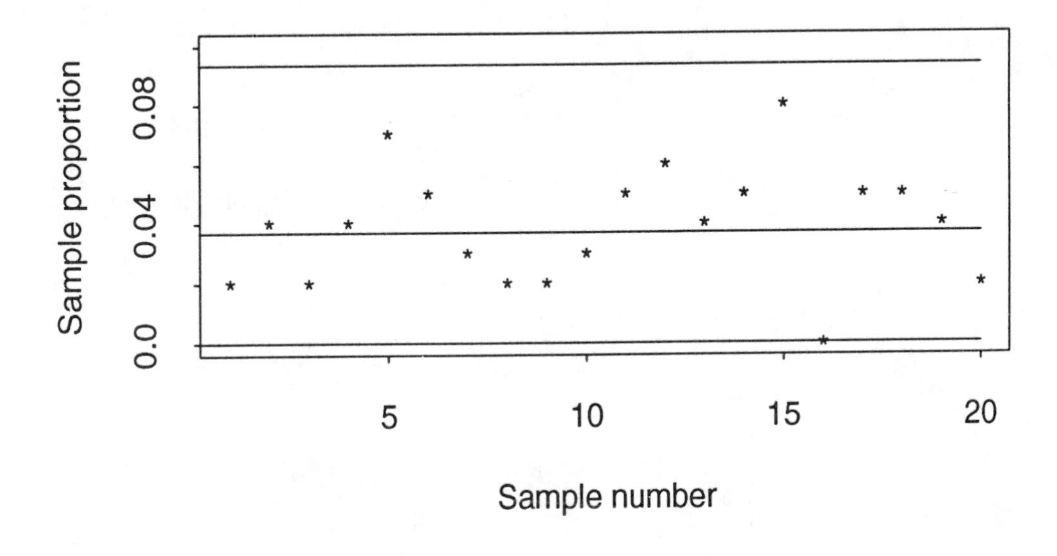

Figure 14.5: Control chart for the proportion defective for Exercise 14.9.

14.13 From Table 14, the tolerance limits are

$$\bar{x} \pm Ks = 52,800 \pm 3.457(4600)$$

or, from 36,897.8 to 68,702.2 . This means that with 95 percent confidence, 99 percent of the pieces will have a yield stress between 36,897.8 and 68,702.2 psi.

14.17 (a) Since the lot size is very large, we can use the binomial distribution. Thus, we need the probability of three or fewer for a binomial distribution with $p = .15$ and $n = 50$ to determine the probability of accepting a lot when the true proportion defective is .15. This is given by

$$\binom{50}{0}(.15)^0(.85)^{50} + \binom{50}{1}(.15)^1(.85)^{49}$$

$$+\binom{50}{2}(.15)^2(.85)^{48} + \binom{50}{3}(.15)^3(.85)^{47}$$

$$= 2.9576 \times 10^{-4} + 2.6097 \times 10^{-3} + 0.011283 + 0.031858 = 0.046047.$$

If the true proportion of defectives is .04, the probability of rejecting is

$$1 - \binom{50}{0}(.04)^0(.96)^{50} - \binom{50}{1}(.04)^1(.96)^{49} - \binom{50}{2}(.04)^2(.96)^{48}$$

$$-\binom{50}{3}(.04)^3(.96)^{47} = 1 - .86087 = .13913.$$

(b) Using the Poisson appproximation, when the true proportion is .15, the expected number of defectives in 50 is $50(.15) = 7.5$. Interpolating in Table 2, we see that the probability of 3 or less defectives is .059. The expected number of defectives when the true proportion is .04 is $50(.04) = 2$. From Table 2, the probability of three or fewer is .857, so the probability of more than 3 is $1 - .8574 = .143$.

14.21 (a) Using the hypergeometric distribution

$$L(.10) = \frac{\binom{10}{0}\binom{90}{10} + \binom{10}{1}\binom{90}{9}}{\binom{100}{10}}$$

$$= \frac{(90!/80!10!) + 10(90!/9!81!)}{100!/90!10!} = .330476 + .407995 = .73847$$

(b)

$$L(.10) = \binom{10}{0}(.10)^0(.90)^10 + \binom{10}{1}(.10)^1(.90)^9$$

$$= (.90)^9(.90 + 10(.10)) = .73610.$$

(c)

$$L(p) \;=\; (1-p)^9(1-p+10p) = (1-p)^9(1+9p)$$

The calculations for the plot of the OC curve are in Table 14.3. The plot of the OC curve is given in Figure 14.6.

(d) $AOQ \;=\; pL(p)$. The calculations for the plot are also shown in Table 14.3 and the plot is given in Figure 14.7.

Table 14.3. Calculation of the OC curve and AOQ curve for Exercise 14.21.

p	$L(p)$	AOQ	p	$L(p)$	AOQ
0.03	0.9655	0.0290	0.33	0.1080	0.0356
0.06	0.8824	0.0529	0.36	0.0764	0.0275
0.09	0.7746	0.0697	0.39	0.0527	0.0206
0.12	0.6583	0.0790	0.42	0.0355	0.0149
0.15	0.5443	0.0816	0.45	0.0233	0.0105
0.18	0.4392	0.0791	0.48	0.0148	0.0071
0.21	0.3464	0.0727	0.51	0.0091	0.0046
0.24	0.2673	0.0642	0.54	0.0054	0.0029
0.27	0.2019	0.0545	0.57	0.0031	0.0018
0.30	0.1493	0.0448	0.60	0.0017	0.0010

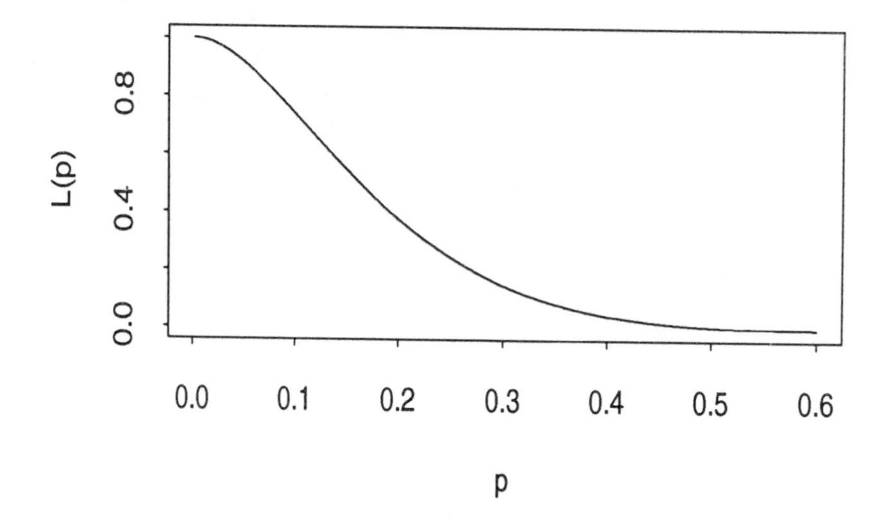

Figure 14.6: OC curve for Exercise 14.21.

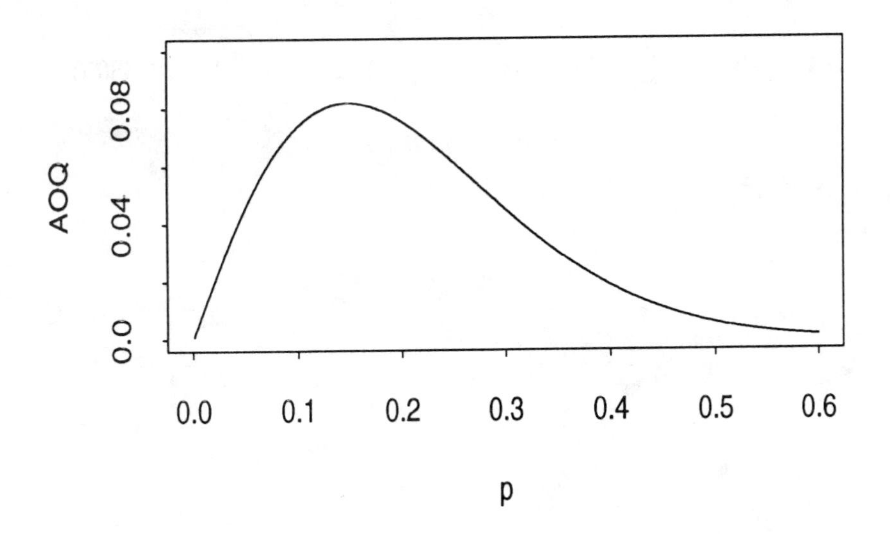

Figure 14.7: AOQ curve for Exercise 14.21.

14.25 The producer's risk is

$$P(5 \text{ or more in the 1-st sample})$$

$$+P(1 \text{ in the 1-st sample}) \cdot P(5 \text{ or more in the 2-nd sample})$$

$$+P(2 \text{ in the 1-st sample}) \cdot P(4 \text{ or more in the 2-nd sample})$$

$$+P(3 \text{ in the 1-st sample}) \cdot P(3 \text{ or more in the 2-nd sample})$$

$$+P(4 \text{ in the 1-st sample}) \cdot P(2 \text{ or more in the 2-nd sample})$$

or

$$(1 - .9873) + (.3431)(.0641) + (.2669)(.1807) + (.1285)(.3805)$$

$$+ (.0429)(.6195) = .1584.$$

14.29 Using the formulas in Section 14.9 of the book,

$$a_n = -1.67 + (.186)n$$

$$r_n = 2.14 + (.186)n$$

The acceptance and rejection numbers for 10 trials are given in Table 14.8. The sample would be rejected on the 8-th trial.

Table 14.8. Acceptance and rejection numbers. Exercise 4.29.

Trial no.	Acceptance number	Rejection number
1	-	-
2	-	-
3	-	3
4	-	3
5	-	4
6	-	4
7	-	4
8	-	4
9	0	4
10	0	5

14.33 If p is 0.02, then the central line is at 0.02, the

$$LCL = p - 3\sqrt{p(1-p)/200} \;=\; 0.02 - 3\sqrt{0.02(1-0.02)/200} \;=\; -0.0097$$

which is taken to be 0, and

$$UCL = p + 3\sqrt{p(1-p)/200} \;=\; 0.02 + 3\sqrt{0.02(1-0.02)/200} \;=\; 0.0497$$

The control chart is given in Figure 14.8. There are five points that are outside the control limits, so the standard is not being met.

14.37 The $n = 50$ transformed observations $y = \ln x$ have $\bar{y} \;=\; 8.846$ and $s_y = 1.0293$ From Table 14 $K \;=\; 1.996$ so the 95 percent tolerance limits on proportion $P = .90$ for the transformed observations are

$$\bar{x} \pm Ks = 8.846 \pm 1.996(1.2093)$$

or 6.7915 to 10.9005. Converting these to the original scale, the tolerance limits are exp(6.7915) to exp(10.9005) or 890 to 54,203. This means that, with 95 percent confidence, 90 percent of the inter-request times will be between 890 and 54,203.

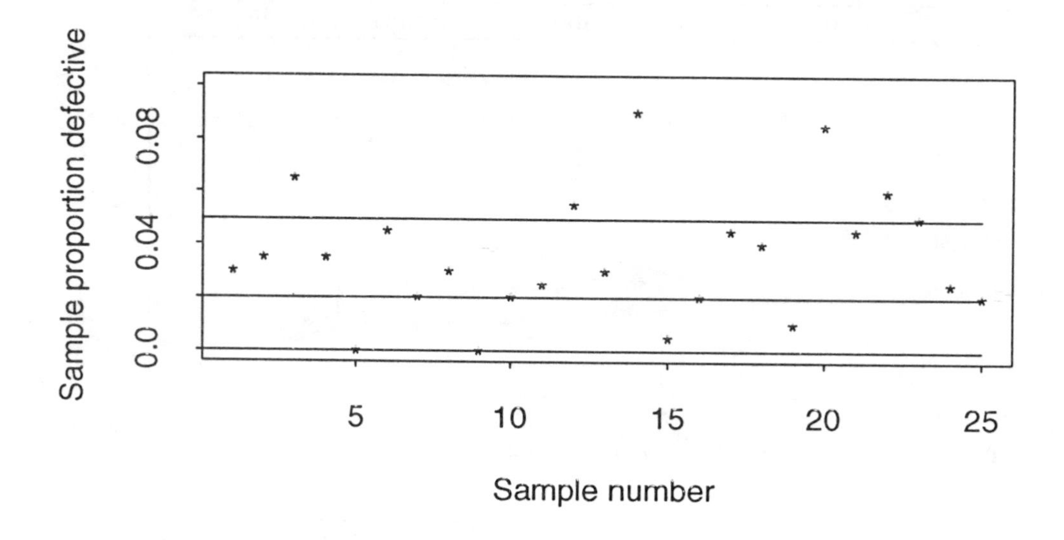

Figure 14.8: Control chart for the fraction defective for Exercise 14.33.

14.41 The code letter is F. The sampling plan is to randomly select 20 items, accept if there are 2 or fewer defectives, and reject if there are 3 or more.

14.45 The sample mean and sample standard deviation are $\bar{x} = 2.5064$ and $s = .0022$.

(a)

$$\hat{C}_p = \frac{USL - LSL}{6s} = \frac{2.516 - 2.496}{6(.0022)} = 1.515.$$

(b)

$$\begin{aligned}\hat{C}_{pk} &= \frac{\min(\bar{x} - LSL,\ USL - \bar{x})}{3s} \\ &= \frac{\min(2.5064 - 2.4960,\ 2.5160 - 2.5064)}{3(.0022)} \\ &= \frac{\min(.0104,\ .0096)}{3(.0022)} = 1.45\end{aligned}$$

Chapter 15

APPLICATIONS TO RELIABILITY AND LIFE TESTING

15.1 Since this is a series system , we need to find R such that

$$R^8 = .95 \quad \text{so} \quad R = (.95)^{1/8} = .9936.$$

15.5 (a) We have that

$$f(t) = Z(t)\, exp\,[-\int_0^t Z(t)\, dt\,].$$

where

$$Z(t) = \begin{cases} \beta(1 - t/\alpha) & \text{for } 0 < t < \alpha. \\ 0 & \text{elsewhere.} \end{cases}$$

Thus

$$f(t) = \begin{cases} \beta(1 - t/\alpha)\, exp\,[-\int_0^t \beta(1 - x/\alpha)\, dx\,] & \text{for } 0 < t < \alpha. \\ 0 & \text{elsewhere.} \end{cases}$$

so

$$f(t) = \begin{cases} \beta(1 - t/\alpha)\, exp\,[\,-\beta(t - t^2/(2\alpha)\,)\,] & \text{for } 0 < t < \alpha. \\ 0 & \text{elsewhere.} \end{cases}$$

The distribution function is

$$F(t) = \begin{cases} \int_0^t f(x)\,dx & \text{for } 0 < t < \alpha. \\ \int_0^\alpha f(x)\,dx & \text{for } t > \alpha. \end{cases}$$

or

$$F(t) = \begin{cases} 1 - exp\,[\,-\beta(t - t^2/(2\alpha)\,)\,] & \text{for } 0 < t < \alpha. \\ 1 - exp\,[\,-\alpha\beta/2] & \text{for } t > \alpha. \end{cases}$$

(b) the probability of initial failure is $F(\alpha) = 1 - e^{-\alpha\beta/2}$ as shown in the previous part.

15.9 Using the formula for the mean time between failures

$$\mu_p = \frac{1}{\alpha}(1 + \frac{1}{2} + + \cdots + \frac{1}{n}) = \frac{1}{9 \times 10^{-4}}(1 + \frac{1}{2} + + \cdots + \frac{1}{n}).$$

Since the failure rate is the inverse of the mean time between failures, in this case we require that $\mu_p \geq 1/(4 \times 10^{-4})$. Thus we must find n such that

$$\frac{9}{4} \leq (1 + \frac{1}{2} + \cdots + \frac{1}{n}).$$

A trial and error search yields $n = 5$ and the failure rate is

$$\frac{9.0 \times 10^{-4}}{2.2833} = 3.94 \times 10^{-4}.$$

15.13 (a) The probability of failure on any trial is p and the probability of no failure is $1 - p$ provided failure has not occurred previously. thus, failure on the x'th trial means no failure for $x - 1$ trials and then a failure. Since the trials are independent

$$f(x) = (1-p)^{x-1}\, p \quad \text{for} \quad x = 1, 2, 3, \ldots$$

(b)

$$\begin{aligned} F(x) &= \sum_{i=1}^{x} (1-p)^{i-1} p = p \sum_{i=0}^{x-1} (1-p)^i \\ &= p \frac{1-(1-p)^x}{p} = 1-(1-p)^x \quad \text{for} \quad x = 1, 2, 3, \cdots \end{aligned}$$

(c) The probability that the switch survives 2,000 cycles is

$$1 - F(2000) = (1 - 6 \times 10^{-4})^{2000} = .301.$$

15.17 (a)

$$\begin{aligned} T_r &= \sum_{i=1}^{r} t_i + (n-r) t_r \\ &= 211 + 350 + 384 + 510 + 539 + 620 + 715 = 3,329. \end{aligned}$$

Since $\chi^2_{.975}$ with 14 degrees of freedom is 5.629 and $\chi^2_{.025}$ with 14 degrees of freedom is 26.119, the 95 percent confidence interval is

$$\frac{2 \cdot 3329}{26.119} < \mu < \frac{2 \cdot 3329}{5.629}$$

or

$$254.9 < \mu < 1,182.8$$

(b) The null hypothesis is $\mu = 500$ and the alternative is $\mu \neq 500$. Since $\chi^2_{.05}$ with 14 degrees of freedom is 23.658 and $\chi^2_{.95}$ with 14 degrees of freedom is 6.571, we reject the null hypothesis at the .10 level if

$$T_r < \frac{1}{2}\mu_0\chi^2_{.95} = \frac{1}{2}(500)(6.571) = 1,642.75$$

or if

$$T_r > \frac{1}{2}\mu_0\chi^2_{.05} = \frac{1}{2}(500)(23.685) = 5,921.25$$

Since T_r = 3,329 , we cannot reject the null hypothesis at the .10 level of significance.

15.21 The total time on test is $T = (200)(3000) = 6 \times 10^5$ and the number of failures is $k = 0$. Since $\chi^2_{.05} = 5.991$ for 2 degrees of freedom, the approximate 95 percent lower confidence bound is

$$\frac{2T}{\chi^2_{.05}} = \frac{2(6 \times 10^5)}{5.991} = 2.003 \times 10^5$$

15.25 Suppose T has the Weibull distribution with parameters α and β. In the text it was shown that

$$E(T) = \frac{1}{\alpha^{1/\beta}}\Gamma(1 + \frac{1}{\beta})$$

Since $Var(T) = E(T^2) - [E(T)]^2$, we must find $E(T^2)$. The Weibull density is

$$\alpha\beta t^{\beta-1}e^{-\alpha t^\beta}$$

so

$$E(T^2) = \int_0^\infty t^2\alpha\beta t^{\beta-1}e^{-\alpha t^\beta}\, dt.$$

Let $u = \alpha t^\beta$. Then

$$E(T^2) = \frac{1}{\alpha^{2/\beta}}\int_0^\infty u^{2/\beta}e^{-u}du = \frac{1}{\alpha^{2/\beta}}\Gamma(1 + \frac{2}{\beta})$$

so that

$$Var(T) = \frac{1}{\alpha^{2/\beta}}\Gamma(1+\frac{2}{\beta}) - (\frac{1}{\alpha^{1/\beta}}\Gamma(1+\frac{1}{\beta}))^2$$
$$= \frac{1}{\alpha^{2/\beta}} \cdot [\, \Gamma(1+\frac{2}{\beta}) - (\Gamma(1+\frac{1}{\beta}))^2 \,]$$

15.29 The mean time between failures for a series system is:

$$MTBF = \frac{1}{\frac{1}{\mu_1}+\frac{1}{\mu_2}+\frac{1}{\mu_3}+\frac{1}{\mu_4}+\frac{1}{\mu_5}+\frac{1}{\mu_6}}$$

$$= \frac{1}{1.8+2.4+2.0+1.3++3.0+1.5} = .0833 \text{ thousand hours}$$

or 83.3 hours.

15.33 The probability the circuit will perform at least 100 hours is 1 minus the probability that it fails before 100 hours. Since

$$1 - F(100) = 1 - (1 - e^{-\alpha(100)^{\beta}})$$

$\hat{\alpha} = .0000909$ and $\hat{\beta} = 1.3665$, we estimate this probability by

$$e^{-\hat{\alpha}(100)^{\hat{\beta}}} = e^{-(.0000909)(100)^{1.3665}} = .9520.$$